The Churches of the New Testament

A 13 Lesson Study On The Subject of The Churches of the New Testament.

This is the eleventh annual Northeast Florida lectureship held at the Wesconnett church of Christ in Jacksonville, Florida.

Editor
Johnie Scaggs, Jr.

INTRODUCTION

A study of the churches of the New Testament is extremely important for every age, but especially this age. We live in an age of unbelief. More and more, we are seeing members of the body of Christ turn their back on the New Testament church. They are consumed with the new age movement that calls for all religious groups to accept everyone regardless of their differing beliefs.

A true understanding and a love for the New Testament church will help turn back the tide. It will only be by a new awakening to the true church that we can save the world of today and tomorrow.

It is to this end that we place this book into your hands, hoping and praying you will use it to the glory of God. Teach others about the importance of the New Testament church, for it is only through the true church salvation is offered.

To the glory of Him
Johnie Scaggs, Jr.

TABLE OF CONTENTS

The Church in Corinth
      Steve Atnip 4
The Church in Ephesus
      Allen Cross 16
The Church in Galatia
      Miles Peeples 26
The Church in Jerusalem
      Ryan Frederick 42
The Church in Laodicea
      Curtis Cates 54
The Church in Pergamos
      Tom Bright 64
The Church in Philadelphia
      Robert Taylor, Jr 76
The Church in Philippi
      Raymond Sieg 86
The Church in Colosse
      Robert Taylor, Jr 96
The Church in Sardis
      Tom Bright 108
The Church in Smyrna
      Charles Or, Sr 122
The Church in Thessalonica
      Curtis Cates 130
The Church in Thyatira
      Ryan Tuten 142

The Church at Corinth

The Churches of the New Testament

INTRODUCTION

When one looks at any of the inspired letters to the churches, it is easy to very accurately pick apart their faults, since the inspiration of heaven makes their faults and their problems abundantly clear, but let us consider these books from another perspective. Suppose we were looking at the cities in which these churches were established as if we were examining those communities before these churches were actually planted there, with a view to beginning a congregation in that place.

What if today we were planning to begin a work in Las Vegas, Nevada? What would be the difficulties we might face? What problems might the people face in coming to Christ or living for Christ, after living in the extraordinarily immoral environment of gambling with its associated vices and immoral behavior? After a few years had passed and a new preacher moved into the city, one of the first things with which he would be confronted is the need to assess the impact of the church on the community, and the community on the church.

When we read the letters written to Corinth, we are reading the assessment of heaven as it revealed both what the church at Corinth was doing for its community as well as how Corinthian Christians had been impacted by their community. The study of this assessment should not interest us as simply a book of faults. It is easy to point out the multiple ways Corinthian saints failed to live up to the gospel's requirements, but it is also beneficial for us to study not only the "what" but also the "why" of their failures. These books also show the answers to dealing with the failed attitudes exhibited in sinful behaviors when the church relates to its community.

Thus, for the sake of this lesson, we divide our thoughts into four considerations: the assessment of the city's culture; an assessment of where the church failed to confront and overcome the sinful values of the city; a look at the principles Paul uses to overcome their errors and complete Corinth's arsenal of spiritual weaponry essential to meeting their God-given purpose as a church; and finally we shall note Corinth's repentance and the impact on its world in spite of its earlier failures.

ASSESSING THE CORINTHIAN CULTURE

The city of Corinth was unique in some ways among the cities of its time. Corinth had an early and illustrious history as a Grecian city, but in 146 BC, Grecian Corinth had been completely destroyed and left in ruins for about a hundred years. In 44 BC, Julius Caesar rebuilt the city based on a Roman model, and repopulated it with freed slaves and Roman veterans (as payment for their service to the empire). It had been rebuilt by Caesar because of its strategic location on the isthmus that joined the two seas between Italy in the West and Asia in the east. The trade between these points made Corinth exceptionally wealthy. Corinth also hosted the Panhellenic or Isthmian games every two years (Okure 108) at the temple of Poseidon. In order to accommodate the tremendous trade and nationalities that came to the city, Corinth had erected many Pagan temples to their Greek, Roman and Egyptian gods: besides Poseidon, there were temples to Aphrodite, Apollo, Athena, Asclepius, Zeus, Donysius, and Isis (Okure 109). Included in the temples were large rooms for banqueting, where the idol gods were honored with the eating of sacrificial foods. These banqueting halls were also used by the citizens for both personal and political needs, so one might be called to eat at the temple banquet, but not necessarily just for a religious occasion. However, there was no thought of division between church and state, and eating at the temple might rightly be construed as honoring the deity of that temple. Several invitations to such affairs have been discovered in the archaeological excavations in the city, which show the varieties of banqueting uses of the temples.

These temples were rife with immoral conduct. The combination of sexually immoral conduct with religion was a feature of the Pagan temples. Sexual immorality with the male and female prostitutes of a temple was considered holy and sacred, and a great source of monetary income for the temples. A Gentile reared in this environment saw such immoral religious activity as a valid worship act just as a Christian thinks of partaking of the Lord's Supper on Sunday. Sexual license in the temple context was expected and honored.

Alongside the temple culture were also many religious preachers and philosophers of every stripe. Among those were Stoics, Epicureans and Cynics, who could slice and dice philosophical thought to encourage any and every kind of immoral lifestyle: from feasting to fasting, from debauchery to abstinence, from reasons to hold to life to advocating suicide. Any taste that might appeal to human vanity, greed, passion, or even some modicum of restraint, found its voice and advocacy in Corinth's culture. Such cultured knowledge, especially from the great philosophers, was considered the pinnacle of human wisdom. To appeal to such wisdom was often the end to all argument. To think outside such philosophy was the height of foolishness in the mind of the Corinthians, much like today when a man rejects organic evolution in favor of Biblical creation.

In addition, while there was great wealth in the city, wealth alone did not insure your status. Capitalist cultures like ours in America are largely based on income levels which determine a man's status in society. Corinth was not a city wherein a person's status was based on monetary achievement in life. The status of people was determined more by two things: a system of patronage, where the wealthy, connected Patron was the only means of advancement in society; and secondly, having your own little group under you who looked to you for advancement in society (Mitchell, 251). In other words, the one with whom you were identified signaled your status. Even a slave rightly connected with a powerful patron assumed status over a wealthy man with no such connections. Also, the greater the number under you looking to you for patronage, the greater was your own status in society.

Finally, we would note that there was a Jewish presence in Corinth. This synagogue had been the voice for advocating and defending the one God of heaven against Pagan polytheism, Jehovah's moral codes versus the debauched behavior of Satanic Paganism, and a promised coming of their Messianic King and kingdom to the Corinthian community. This community of Jewish culture had attracted Greek hearers to its message (Acts 18:4) as it had across the Roman world. Any challenge to their status or position in the Gentile community would be met with fierce opposition.

With this elemental picture of the culture of Corinth, we note that in Acts 18, Paul came to Corinth and established a church of Jesus Christ. The books addressed to the Corinthian congregation are a heavenly assessment of what happened between the church and its host community.

HOW WAS THE CHURCH AFFECTED BY THE CULTURE AND WHAT WAS HEAVEN'S RESPONSE?

After Paul left Corinth, he sent back at least two letters. (Some have postulated a need for at least four letters from Paul; we remain open to such, but are presently unconvinced). These two letters point out the impact the culture of Corinth had on the church.

Status Seeking

We note that as in Corinthian culture, so in the church, men had begun to align themselves with certain leaders and teachers in the church, in an attempt to gain status in the congregation (1 Cor. 1:11-17). Such carnal attitudes are still seen today in mission efforts when status in the church is often sought in association with the missionary or some other respected teacher. The church for many such men gives them status when they have none in the world about them, and the means used is to attach themselves to men of status within the church to elevate themselves. Paul refers to this attitude as one of carnality (1 Cor. 3:1-3). To this Paul responded that the only elevated person in the church is Jesus Christ and that it is into Him that we are baptized and not into any man (1 Cor. 1:13-17). To act otherwise is to destroy the unity of the body of Christ.

Even in the Lord's Supper, as with the pagan temples, the "haves" associated with the other "haves," leaving out the "have not's," and making the communion a common meal such as those in Pagan temple worship. Paul remonstrated strongly against this abuse pointing out that this is communion, not a common meal for filling hunger and showing status. This sacred supper was a focus on Christ, not on their need for status and favor with those who could benefit them (1 Cor. 11:20-34). Leave pagan practices and Corinthian culture out of Christianity.

They continued their intent on the elevation of self even in the use of spiritual gifts in the assembly as seen in I Corinthians, chapter 14. For them, certain spiritual gifts were of greater status than others. Paul pointed out that the assembly is not about spiritual gifts which were to cease in the church (1 Cor. 13:8-10), but was about what spiritual gifts provided: edification, exhortation and comfort to God's family (1 Cor. 14:3). This is a sorely needed lesson for those today who hold spiritual gifts as a matter of status, stating that spiritual gifts are proof of who is really spiritual today. Such attitude is self-elevation over the purposes of the gifts, and a denial of the plain teaching that these gifts were to cease when the complete will of God had been given to man.

Philosophy and Rhetoric

We note also the effect of philosophy and academic rhetoric on the members of the Corinthian church. The cross of Christ was first presented by Paul without any wisdom of men or rhetorical device, as the pinnacle of the wisdom of God in His righteous dealings with men (1 Cor. 2:1-2). To the Greeks, this gospel was foolishness; to the Jews this gospel was a stumbling block (1 Cor. 1:23), for its exaltation of a man who had died a criminal death as the Messianic King of Israel. In both cases each philosophy questioned the need for a crucified Christ, while rejecting the Holy Spirit's divine interpretation of the Old Testament Messianic mystery passages as having been fulfilled by a crucified Messiah (1 Cor. 2:7-13).

Paul responded that even the foolishness of God is wiser than all the wisdom and philosophy of man (1 Cor. 1:25). What the Greek saw as weakness was actually God's power at work in redemption, giving to man the salvation no power on earth could give apart from the crucified Christ (1 Cor. 1:25, 30).

To the Jew, Paul pointed out that the prophetic Messianic passages of the Old Testament were written as mysteries (1 Cor. 1:7) to keep the princes of this world in the dark as to God's plans. Paul stated, "none of the princes of this world knew: for had they known it, they would not have crucified the Lord of glory" (1 Cor. 2:8). Also, the Jew should accept that the same Holy Spirit who wrote the original Old Testament mystery prophesies and had searched the mind of God as to their meaning, had divulged that prophetic interpretation to inspired men. These men were above the judgment of uninspired, uninformed men who were functioning from a carnal mindset and not a Spirit-taught one (1 Cor. 2:9-16).

Paul further pointed out he had intentionally not preached the gospel to them at the first with academic philosophical rhetoric because he wanted them to be moved by the simple Spirit-inspired, Spirit-confirmed message of the gospel, rather than the high-sounding philosophical rhetoric of the world (1 Cor. 2:1-5). Philosophical rhetoric is reproducible in each age by men of earthly wisdom; the gospel was confirmed once for all by unimaginable miraculous divine power. They should stay by the power of God, something human philosophy cannot ever begin to match.

In addition, philosophy struck at the very core of Christianity's hope. Some among them questioned the very possibility of a resurrection from the dead. They philosophized that it could not occur (1 Cor. 15:12), asking how life after death was possible and with what body the dead return (1 Cor. 15:35). For some among them, philosophy had stripped away their hope.

To this Paul responded that the fact of the resurrection was not a philosophy but an empirical truth verified by the testimony of over 500 eyewitnesses at one time in addition to the testimony of the 12 apostles and Paul (1 Cor. 15:5-9). Again, Paul points out that life comes from death every time you plant a seed in the ground (1 Cor. 15:36). Only a fool sees such obvious evidence and still denies that life cannot come from death. Further, the body that comes to life after you plant that seed is one which God gives to it to inhabit a spiritual world which this fleshly body cannot ever enter or inhabit (1 Cor. 15:37-50).

In the realm of moral teaching, philosophy had advanced its cause by a platitude: "meats for the belly and the belly for meats" (1 Cor. 6:13). Since the belly's appetite was for meats, and its purpose is filled when it consumes meat, one should fill its appetite by giving it meats. Likewise, since the body has appetite for fornication, filling that appetite is as natural as filling your belly with food. Both are capacities and appetites within the body, and thus filling them at will is perfectly acceptable. Some of the brethren were enamored of this doctrine and imbibed at will. One had even taken his father's wife and the brethren were puffed up and had allowed this fornicator to continue among them (1 Cor. 5:1-2).

Paul responded that the body was never intended for fornication, but God had made the body for himself (1 Cor. 6:13). If you wish to use the body for its true intent, then honorably serve and glorify God in moral Christian living (1 Cor. 6:20). A passion of man should never be used as an excuse to live or act outside of that greater purpose of honoring God. Further, the church should exclude such brethren from their fellowship and turn them over to Satan for the destruction of the flesh, so their spirits might be saved (1 Cor. 5: 4-13).

Philosophy again struck at the heart of the saints in regard to eating meats offered to idols. The argument was that if you knew that an idol was nothing, then eating meats offered to idols could not be wrong (1 Cor. 8:4). This doctrine only took into regard the mind of the one partaking without regard to any other persons affected. The principle of earthly wisdom was that personal liberty was not to be bound by any rule (1 Cor. 8:9).

Paul replied with heavenly wisdom that liberty used in such a way as to become a stumbling block to others is a sin against Christ (1 Cor. 8:12), and the purpose of the kingdom is the salvation of its members, not the granting of personal liberty for selfish purposes. Use liberty in Christ to expedite the cause of redemption and personally build up the members of the congregation (1 Cor. 10:23).

Moral Living

Alongside philosophy, the temple culture itself was strong in Corinth. The immoralities offered at the temples along with the meats had a strong impact on the community's culture and consequently in the church.

Some were still eating the meats with conscience of the idol (1 Cor. 8:7). In addition, there was strong impetus to engage in fornication as had been the custom in earlier Paganism (1 Cor. 6:13-20). Added to this were the normal pressures of marriage and family among unbelieving and believing mates exacerbated by persecution (1 Cor. 7:26).

Paul responds to weak saints that partaking in the pagan temple feasts was fellowshipping demons who were behind the pagan practices of worship to false gods (1 Cor. 10:20). Further, when they entered into fornication with prostitutes, their bodies were being joined as one with those prostitutes. Saints who are a part of the body of Christ should never join what is a part of God's body to the body of another in an evil act. Remember, our bodies are God's temple and He cannot dwell where immorality abides (1 Cor. 6:15-19). One must choose between God's indwelling Spirit and immorality's pleasures. The two cannot co-exist.

To help in the avoidance of such fornicative practices, Paul answers some of the questions put to him by the brethren in Corinth. During the present distress, Paul advised against marriage, but said if a person needed to, they should marry. Both partners were not to withhold intimacy from one another (1 Cor. 7:2-9). The persecutions, however, had created a stress which was affecting even Christian marriages (1 Cor. 7:26). Paul encourages saints to remain married, even to unbelieving mates (1 Cor. 7:10-27). He goes on to point out to them that these pressures will not always be a part of their lives, but the fashion of the world would change eventually (1 Cor. 7:29-31).

Judaism

Judaism was also making its inroads into the church (2 Cor. 3:7-18). Judaistic teachers had re-entered the picture stressing the keeping and proclamation of Mosaic law as necessary to full Christian doctrine and practice. Some of these teachers were pulling the Corinthian saints away from the pristine Christian teaching Paul had given them from the beginning (2 Cor. 11:3-4). The ancient quality of Judaism reaching back to Moses and the law at Mt. Sinai appealed to many, even as it does today.

Paul's response to this was to point out that Judaism's glory could not compare to the glory of the cross (1 Cor 3:6-18). Judaism's glory was fading from the days of its inception with Moses, while the glory of Christianity burned with an eternal light. Judaism was a covenant of death, while Christianity was a covenant of life. Judaism was veiled as to its greatest meanings of Messiah and His kingdom, while Christianity was the Spirit's fulfillment of the Old Testament prophecies. In Judaism the hearer's heart was veiled to the intent and purposes of God in Christ. In Christianity that veil is removed and the glory of God is revealed in the person of Christ, whose glory is reflected into eternity by those who come to God through Him and change their lives into the image of Christ.

CORINTH'S RESPONSE TO PAUL'S FIRST LETTER

While the culture at Corinth had made inroads into the Corinthian congregation, the same word which had originally won their hearts to Christ, still held great power in their hearts. After Paul's original letter to Corinth in which he addressed their failures in the gospel, Paul notes in his second letter that these saints responded with the same fervor which began their walk with Christ. In the matter of the brother living in fornication with his father's wife Paul wrote, "For behold this selfsame thing, that ye sorrowed after a godly sort, what carefulness it wrought in you, yea, what clearing of yourselves, yea, what indignation, yea, what fear, yea, what vehement desire, yea, what zeal, yea, what revenge! In all things ye have approved yourselves to be clear in this matter" (2 Cor. 7:11). Speaking of the whole tenor of their response to the first letter, a deeply concerned Apostle Paul again writes with a sense of exuberant joy, "Therefore we were comforted in your comfort: yea, and exceedingly the more joyed we for the joy of Titus, because his spirit was refreshed by you all. For if I have boasted any thing to him of you, I am not ashamed; but as we spake all things to you in truth, even so our boasting, which I made before Titus, is found a truth. And his inward affection is more abundant toward you, whilst he remembereth the obedience of you all, how with fear and trembling ye received him. I rejoice therefore that I have confidence in you in all things" (2 Cor. 7:13-16).

Boasting of them? Confidence concerning them in all things? This is the impact of the word on the hearts of truth-loving saints, even in the midst of a world that for a season had an impact on their Christianity. If saints today will but hear the word with tender hearts, even though the world has crushed their hopes, brought some to immorality, at times overcome them with its passion, philosophy and rhetoric and even if ancient shadowy religion shall beckon from afar, Corinth cries to our hearts, "Yet, there is hope." Christianity is stronger; Christ is truly risen, giving us the hope that is greater than all the world has to offer; Christianity shines brighter than all; and the image of Christ is within the grasp of every man and woman.

CONCLUSION

As these letters conclude their inspired assessment of the church at Corinth, there are still false teachers to be dealt with (and Paul would deal with them), but the congregation had restored their reputation as the sons and daughters of God in the midst of a world gone mad with passion and pride. Their light was shining brightly and the Corinthian congregation set forth not the brightness of a bygone fading glory of Judaism with its law on tables of stone; but in Corinth, Zion's city was set on a hill blazing forth in the radiant splendor of the gospel of Christ with the Spirit's inspired message and the glorious image of Jesus written deeply in the hearts of its citizens. When each of the congregations of our Lord today receives their assessment by the word, may each rise to the occasion as did Corinth and zealously repent from evil passions and the wisdom of this world. Then may we stand as brightly as did Corinth when the eternal word exposed their error and called effectively for their change into the eternal and glorious image of God's dear Son.

STUDY QUESTIONS

1. When had the new city of Corinth been built, and by whom?
2. What games did Corinth host and in what temple?
3. Name some of the pagan gods who had temples erected to their honor in Corinth.
4. Was there division between religion and state in Corinth?
5. How was a person's status determined in Corinth?
6. How did the Greek and the Jew look at the crucifixion of Christ?
7. How was status determined by the Corinthian Christians in the assembly of the church?
8. How did Paul respond to the philosophical attack on the resurrection?
9. How was Christian liberty to be used?
10. What verses show how the Corinthians responded to Paul's first letter?

WORKS CITED

Mitchell, Nathan. "Paul's Eucharistic Theology." Worship 83.3 (2009): 250-262.

Okure, Teresa. ""The Ministry of Reconciliation" (2 Cor 5:14-21): Paul's Key to the Problem of "the Other" in Corinth." Mission Studies 23.1 (2006): 105-121.

The Church at Ephesus

The Churches OF THE New Testament

INTRODUCTION

The book of Ephesians was written by the apostle Paul. He wrote in Ephesians 1:1, "Paul, an apostle of Jesus Christ by the will of God." In Ephesians 3:1, he penned, "...For this reason, I, Paul, the prisoner of Jesus Christ for you Gentiles". Furthermore, the epistle is Pauline style and form. To "whom" was the book of Ephesians written? The book was written "to the saints who are in Ephesus" (Eph. 1:1). Ephesus was a commercial and religious center. Therein was the temple of Diana {Roman name} or Artemis {Greek name} (Acts 19:35), one of the Seven Wonders of the World. Paul labored there for three years (Acts 18:23;19:41). It was written about 60-63 A.D. Why was the book of Ephesus written? Ephesians is emphasizing the supremacy of the Church of the Christ, the body of which Christ is the head (Eph. 1:22-23). Paul discusses the Church in God's eternal scheme in the first three chapters. In the remainder of the book he discusses how we are to conduct ourselves within the church.

The letter was written from Rome about the year A.D. 62. Although Paul was on trial for his life, he was concerned about the spiritual needs of the churches he had founded. As an apostle, "one sent with a commission", he had an obligation to teach them the Word of God and to seek to build them up in the faith (Eph. 4:11-12).

Ephesians was written after many churches had been founded and after Paul had the opportunity to contemplate the meaning of the new organism that had come into being. This book was intended to inform the Gentiles of their new calling, and it disclosed the mystery of the body of Christ in which there is neither Jew nor Gentile, bond nor free.

Throughout the epistle to the Ephesians, we find the theme of the "oneness" of the Church. The epistle was not directed to novices in the Christian faith, but rather to those who having achieved some maturity in spiritual experience, desired to go on to a fuller knowledge and life in Christ Jesus. Certain themes recur constantly in the book. The sovereign purpose of God in establishing the Church permeates the first half of this epistle (Eph. 1:4-5,9,11,13,20; 2:4—6,10, 3:11) in which the divine plan of redemption is elaborated. In the second half the conduct of the believer is emphasized in the word "walk", which describes his model for conduct (Eph. 4:1,17; 5:1, 8,15) as contrasted with his former behavior in the world (Eph. 2:1). The sphere of the Christians activities is "in heavenly places" (Eph. 1:3, 10, 20; 2:6; 3: 10; 6:12). This is a phrase that refers to a spiritual location rather than a geographical location.

THE ESTABLISHMENT OF THE CHURCH

It was Paul's desire to go into the province of Asia during his second Missionary Journey, but the Holy Spirit prohibited him (Acts 16:6). After founding works at Philippi, Thessalonica, Berea, Athens and Corinth, Paul, on his way back to Syrian Antioch, made a brief stop at Ephesus (Acts 18:18-19). During his week there, he had an opportunity to preach to the Jews in the synagogue. They wanted Paul to stay for a longer period, but he had to leave; he assured them however, that he would return if it were God's will (Acts 18:19-21).

Aquila and Priscilla, who had accompanied Paul from Corinth to Ephesus, remained at Ephesus after Paul sailed to Caesarea. When Apollos, an orator, expositor, and evangelist of the teachings of John the Baptist, came to Ephesus, the couple explained the truth about Christ to him, and he was converted. Apollos then left for a ministry in Corinth (Acts 18:24-28).

Meanwhile, Paul had started out from Antioch on his third journey through Galatia and Phrygia on his way to Asia. After his arrival in Ephesus, his first converts were twelve disciples of John the Baptist, probably so influenced through the ministry of Apollos (Acts 19:1-7).

Accepting an earlier invitation, Paul preached in the local synagogue for the next three months. When public opposition developed, Paul withdrew from the synagogue, taking the converts with him, and continued his ministry for the next two years in the school of Tyrannue. This work was so effective "that all they which dwelt in Asia heard the Word of the Lord Jesus, both Jews and Greeks" (Acts 19:10). It is very plausible that all of the seven churches of Asia (Ephesus, Smyrna, Pergamos, Thyatira, Sardis, Philadelphia and Laodicea; cf. Rev. 2:3) were founded at this time either directly by Paul or indirectly through Paul's associates or converts. Luke recorded: "So mightily grew the word of God and prevailed" (Acts 19:20). Paul himself wrote: "For a great door and effectual is opened unto me, and there are many adversaries" (1 Cor. 16:9).

Opposition came from pagan silversmiths who made their living through the manufacture of miniature statues of Diana and of replicas of her temple (Acts 19:23-41). Paul had already planned to leave Ephesus to visit in Macedonia and Achaia, to return to Jerusalem, and then to sail for Rome; he sent an advance team, but stayed on in Asia "for a season" (Acts 19:21-22). It was at this time that Demetrius, enraged over the decline of Shrine sales, provoked a mob to seize Paul's companions, Gaius and Aristarchus, and to take them before the pagan leaders of Ephesians to the theater. Paul wanted to join his friends in their hour of need, but the believers restrained him from doing so.

When it looked as though the two companions would be executed, the town clerk {or mayor} warned the assembly that their actions would be investigated by Rome, declared that legal channels were open to the silversmiths, and dismissed the assembly.

When the uproar was over, Paul left Ephesus for Macedonia, ending a ministry of about three years in that city (Acts 20:31). Later at Miletus, on his trip to Jerusalem, he counseled the Ephesian elders about their responsibilities to teach the believers and to warn them against the advent of false teachers (Acts 20:17-38). This was his last contact with the Church until the writing of this epistle.

DISTINCTIVE FEATURES OF THE CHURCH

The theme of Ephesians is the Church; however, Paul was not emphasizing the organization of the local church, but the organism of the Universal Church. This was the Church Christ predicted would be built upon his person and redemptive work (cf. Matt. 16:18-21). Paul entitled it the Church (Eph. 1:22;3:10-21). Paul referred to the Universal Church as: His (Christ's) Body (Eph. 4:4), the household of God (Eph. 2:19), the building (Eph. 2:21), and the holy temple in the Lord (Eph. 2:12), an habitation of God (Eph. 2:22), the mystery (Eph. 3:3), the mystery of Christ (Eph. 3:4), the whole family in heaven and earth (Eph. 3:15), the saints (Eph. 4:12), the body of Christ (Eph. 4:12). He also refers to the Church as: The whole body (Eph. 4:16), dear children (Eph. 5:1), children of light (Eph. 5:18), members of His body, of His flesh, and of His bones (Eph. 5:30), and the mystery of the gospel (Eph. 6:19).

Certain key words or phrases were used rather frequently in this book: in (ninety times). "Grace" (thirteen), "Spirit or Spiritual" (thirteen), "body" (eight), "walk" (eight) "heavenly" (five), and "mystery" (five).

Pneumatology is stressed in the book. The personality of the Holy Spirit is seen in the fact that He is holy (Eph. 1:13), that He has wisdom and can reveal truth (Eph. 1:17;3:5). One spirit (Eph. 2:18), the Spirit (Eph. 2:22), He is known as the one Spirit (Eph. 4:4), and the Holy Spirit of God (Eph. 4:30).

The Holy Spirit's works are many: at the moment of faith and obedience, believers were sealed with Him (Eph. 1:13). He is the earnest of their inheritance (Eph. 1:14), by Him believers have access to the father (Eph. 2:18), the church is being built through Him (Eph. 2:22); Spiritual truth has been revealed by Him (Eph. 3:5); believers are strengthened internally by Him (Eph. 3:16). We should be filled with Him (Eph. 5:18), and we should pray in Him (Eph. 6:18). The spirit provides one piece of the Christian armor, the Word of God (Eph. 6:17).

YOU'RE IN THE ARMY NOW!

Sooner or later every believer discovers that the Christian life is a battleground, not a playground, and that he faces an enemy who is much stronger than he is--apart from the Lord. That Paul should use the military to illustrate the believer's conflict with Satan is reasonable. He himself was chained to a Roman soldier (Eph. 6:20), and his readers were certainly familiar with soldiers and the equipment they used. In fact, military illustrations were favorites with Paul (2 Tim. 2:3;4:2;4:7;1 Tim. 6:12;2 Cor. 10:4).

In the closing verses of the letter, Paul discussed four topics so that his readers, by understanding and applying these truths, might walk in victory.

1. THE ENEMY (Eph. 6:10-12)

The intelligence corps plays a vital part in warfare because it enables the officers to know and understand the enemy. Unless we know who the enemy is, where he is, and what he can do, we have a difficult time defeating him. Not only in Ephesians six, but throughout the entire Bible, God instructs us about the enemy, so there is no reason for us to be caught off guard.

Our enemy is the devil. He has many different names. Devil means "accuser" because he accuses God's people day and night before the throne of God (Rev. 12:7-11). Satan means "adversary", because he is the enemy of God. He is also called the "tempter" (Matt. 4:3), a murderer and a liar (John 8:44). He is compared to a lion (1 Pet. 5:6), a serpent (Gen. 3:1; Rev. 12:9). He is said to be an angel of light (2 Cor. 11:13-15), as well as "the god of this age" (2 Cor. 4:4, NIV).

Where did he originate this spirit-creature, that seeks to oppose God and defeat His work? Many students believe that in the original creation, he was "Lucifer, son of the morning", (Isa. 14:12-15), that he was cast down because of his pride and his desire to occupy God's throne. However, "Lucifer" of Isaiah 14:12-15 is not referring to the Devil, but rather to the king of Babylon (Isa. 14:4). Many mysteries are connected with the origin of Satan that have not been revealed to us.

However, what he is doing and where he is going is certainly no mystery! Since he is a created being and not eternal (as God is), he is limited in his knowledge and activity. Unlike God, Satan is not all-knowing, all-powerful or everywhere present. Then how does he accomplish so much in so many different parts of the world? The answer lies in his organized helpers. Paul called them "principalities...powers...ruler...spiritual wickedness in high places" (v. 12). A spiritual battle is going on in this world. We, as God's children are fighting against those principalities, powers, rulers, and those in high places who are spiritually wicked. It is a battle that will continue until the end of time. Satan will not be victorious, but rather the Lord and His children will be the victors.

2. THE EQUIPMENT (Eph. 6:13-17)

Since we are fighting against enemies who are spiritually wicked, we need special equipment both for offense and defense. God has provided the "whole armor" for us, and we dare not omit any part. Satan looks for that unguarded area where he can get a beachhead (Eph. 4:27). Paul commanded his readers to put on the whole armor of God, take the weapons, and withstand Satan. Knowing Christ will be victorious over Satan, and the spiritual armor and weapons are available, by faith we accept what God gives, and go out to meet the foe. The day is evil, and the enemy is evil, but, "if God be for us, who can be against us?" (Rom. 8:31).

3. THE ENERGY (Eph. 6:18-20)

Prayer is the energy that enables the Christian soldier to wear the armor and wield the sword. We cannot fight the battle by our own power no matter how strong we may think we are.

4. THE ENCOURAGEMENT (Eph. 6:21-24)

We are not fighting the battle alone. Other believers stand with us in the fight, and we should be careful to encourage one another. Paul encouraged the Ephesians; Tychicus was an encouragement to Paul (Acts 20:4); and Paul was going to send Tychicus to Ephesus to be an encouragement to them.

CONCLUSION

Paul cautioned the believers that his attempts to put into practice his spiritual position would be done in the midst of spiritual warfare. To understand the attacks of Satan, the believer must put on spiritual armor. The foe of the Christian is not human, but rather our foe is the devil. This armor is defensive in character because the battle will be brought to the believer. It is the believer's responsibility to repel the attacks and to stand his ground. This spiritual armor has six pieces or features of this spiritual armor: Girdle of truth; Breastplate of righteousness; Sandals of peace; and the sword of the spirit, which is the Word of God. In putting on the armor and in withstanding the attacks, the believer must constantly be praying for himself and for other saints.

Paul ended this epistle with a request that the Ephesians pray for him that he might boldly preach the Word during his Roman imprisonment. He informed them that Tychicus would make known the apostle's personal affairs. He concluded with a typical Pauline benediction.

Note the words Paul uses as he closes this letter: Peace – Love – Faith – Grace! Yes, He was a prisoner of Rome. Yet, he was richer than the Emperor! No matter what our circumstances may be, in Jesus Christ, we are "blessed with all spiritual blessings"!

The Church At Ephesus **23**

STUDY QUESTIONS

1. Who wrote the Book of Ephesians?
2. To whom was the Book of Ephesians written?
3. Why was the Book of Ephesians written?
4. Where was the letter written from?
5. What year was the letter written?
6. What Theme runs throughout the Book?
7. Who were Aquila and Priscilla?
8. What was the opposition that came from the silversmith?
9. What are some of the distinctive features of the Ephesian Church?
10. How many pieces of armor did Paul mention?

WORKS CITED

WINKLER Wendell, A study of Ephesians. Life changing studies with an Open Bible, The supremacy of the Church. Winkler Publications, Inc. 2005. Page 4.

TENNEY, Merrill G., New Testament Survey. M.B. FERDMANS PUBLISHING COMPANY 1953. Page 319 – 320.

GROMACK, Robert G., New Testament Survey. Baker Book House, Grand Rapids, Michigan 1974 Page 241 – 244.

WIERSBE, Warren W., BE RICH; An Expository Study of the Epistle to the Ephesians. A division of SP Publications, Inc. Wheaton, Ll. Pages 163-274

The Church at Galatia

INTRODUCTION

When Paul and Barnabas left Antioch of Syria on their first missionary trip, they journeyed to the island of Cyprus. After preaching in Salamis and Paphos, they set sail for the mainland, arriving in Perga of Pamphylia, where they ministered for a short period of time. Leaving Perga, the two missionaries traveled north approximately 80 miles to the city of Antioch in Pisidia. Antioch, Iconium, Lystra, and Derbe were cities located in the Roman province called Galatia. This territory was a political entity used for governance under Roman rule; and within it there were geographical regions which, in years earlier, had been known by other names. However, for the purpose of this lecture, the church in Galatia was made up of the congregations in the center section of what is today Asia Minor or Turkey. In the middle of the first century, it was known as the Roman province of Galatia.

From the inspired history of the establishment of the church in Galatia, found in Acts 13 and 14, many important lessons may be noted. However, in what follows, our exploration will focus on some lessons we may learn from Paul's epistle to the churches in the Roman province of Galatia. In the judgment of the writer, several relevant and timely lessons may be placed before our minds for consideration. Let's take a look at these lessons.

A CONSTANT DANGER

While the probable year in which the Apostle Paul wrote his letter to the Galatians ranges from 49 AD to 57 AD, the more likely date seems to be 53 AD.

In regard to this latter date, Lenski presented the more convincing case. After offering several factors for consideration, he wrote the following conclusion: "The most acceptable date to which we are able to assign Galatians is near April in the year 53 while Paul was at Corinth" (Lenski, 17). Consequently, Paul wrote Galatians no more than eighteen months after visiting the churches of Galatia at the beginning of his second missionary journey. During this short span of time, a percentage of Christians in Galatia had embraced the teachings of the Judaizing heretics. Many others were vulnerable to what these false teachers were saying. The situation was indeed very serious and had arisen in only a few months.

The fact some Galatian Christians turned away so quickly from the true gospel illustrates an important danger constantly facing the church. In a short period of time, it is possible for Christians to swallow a doctrine contrary to what the Lord Jesus Christ has authorized. The Galatians did. The church in our day can also turn away from the gospel, which was completely revealed in the first century.

Why was the false message of the Judaizing teachers dangerous? Speaking briefly, the Judaizers taught that an individual must be circumcised and keep the Law of Moses in order to be saved. Their position may be summarized as follows:

> And certain men came down from Judaea and taught the brethren, saying, Except ye be circumcised after the custom of Moses, ye cannot be saved. And when Paul and Barnabas had no small dissension and questioning with them, the brethren appointed that Paul and Barnabas, and certain other of them, should go up to Jerusalem unto the apostles and elders about this question. They therefore, being brought on their way by the church, passed through both Phoenicia and Samaria, declaring the conversion of the Gentiles: and they caused great joy unto all the brethren. And when they were come to Jerusalem, they were received of the church and the apostles and the elders, and they rehearsed all things that God had done with them. But there rose up certain of the sect of the Pharisees who believed, saying, It is needful to circumcise them, and to charge them to keep the law of Moses (Acts 15:1-5, ASV).

Clearly, their position, keeping of the Law of Moses was as important as believing in and following the Lord Jesus Christ. They did not reject Jesus as the Messiah, the Son of God. Moreover, they did not repudiate the teachings given by Jesus. According to these false teachers, the gospel was to be added to the Old Testament law. Their motto seemed to have been the following: Jesus plus Moses. Also, it must be kept in mind they never gave up their fundamental conviction. To them, one's acceptance with God came as a result of one having earned it through keeping the law. The Galatian letter detailed the danger of such a false message and showed why it was indeed false. One may succinctly say the message of the Judaizing teachers was a perversion of the one, true gospel (Gal. 1:6-7); because it was a perversion, the Jesus-plus-Moses doctrine lost all power unto salvation (Gal. 5:2-4). This was the grave danger presented by the message of the Judaizing heretics. Some of the Christians in Galatia had bought into this perverted gospel, and they had turned away from the true gospel in a very short period of time.

It does not necessarily take a long period of time for a Christian or a congregation to embrace a false doctrine. Like the churches of Galatia, a false doctrine may be accepted in a relatively short period. For example, just a few years ago, almost every congregation across America taught the truth concerning marriage, divorce, and remarriage. They taught only the "innocent party" had the right to remarry and Matthew 19:1-9 applied to all people, whether Christians or not. In only a few years, however, many congregations embraced a doctrine contrary to what the Lord Jesus had given. These congregations, or at least the leadership of these congregations, turned away from walking in the truth and began to follow after a perverted gospel. Indeed, for an individual or a congregation to accept a false doctrine does not always take a long time. It can happen in a very short period of time; this is the grave danger that constantly faces the church of Christ.

A SURE SAFEGUARD

To guard against the danger of embracing a false doctrine, resulting in a turning away from the true gospel, Paul told the Galatians there was a sure safeguard. The most effective safeguard against embracing false doctrine, Paul indicated, was to preach, believe, and obey the true gospel. If a false, perverted gospel was not allowed to be preached, and if only the true gospel was preached and followed, then the danger of turning away into damnable error was eminently decreased. Paul wrote the following:

> I marvel that ye are so quickly removing from him that called you in the grace of Christ unto a different gospel; which is not another gospel only there are some that trouble you, and would pervert the gospel of Christ. But though we, or an angel from heaven, should preach unto you any gospel other than that which we preached unto you, let him be anathema. As we have said before, so say I now again, if any man preacheth unto you any gospel other than that which ye received, let him be anathema (ASV Gal.1:6-9).

In this passage, the apostle stated the genuine, authentic gospel had been preached to them, and they had received it. Primarily, Paul referred to his labors among them during his first and second missionary journeys. In Galatians 3:1, Paul said, "O foolish Galatians, who did bewitch you, before whose eyes Jesus Christ was openly set forth crucified?" In Greek the verb, "was openly set forth," is an aorist indicative passive, which means the truth about Jesus Christ had been preached to them at a point in the past. There is little doubt Paul spoke in large measure about his own preaching and teaching. He preached the truth of the gospel during his first and second missionary journeys. Moreover, the gospel Paul preached never included the observance of the law of Moses as necessary to salvation. What the apostle said about his preaching in Corinth was also the case in Galatia. Concerning his preaching in Corinth, Paul said the following: "For I determined not to know anything among you, save Jesus Christ, and him crucified" (1 Cor. 2:2).

To preach Jesus included speaking about His authority; that is, His Lordship. Since Jesus Christ was Lord, having been given all authority in heaven and on earth, whatever He required of the Galatians became a law unto them. They were to keep the law of Christ. After the death, burial, and resurrection of Jesus, Jews and all other individuals were no longer subject to the law of Moses as the way to be pleasing to God. In preaching the true gospel, Paul preached Jesus instead of Moses. He taught the commandments of the Lord Jesus Christ, never the commandments of Moses. This was the message that had been preached to them, and the message they had received. The word "accursed" is an interesting word. Lenski makes the following observation:

The Hebrew cherem = something that is removed from the possession or use of men and set aside for God, either as an object upon which God's wrath rests or an object that is dedicated to God as a gift. Hellenic Greek used anaqema for the former in the sense of "accursed," anaqhma for the latter (Lenski, 40).

In Galatians 1:8-9, Paul used the Greek word anaqema, and in doing so, he indicated it was a damnable thing to preach a perverted gospel as though it were the true gospel that had been preached from the beginning. Even an angel would be under the wrath of God if he proclaimed a perverted gospel. The gospel cannot be altered. It cannot be changed. Its integrity must be maintained.

Today many men fail to maintain the integrity of the gospel. They pervert it by making changes. For example, relative to the person of Jesus, some people say He is only a mere man like any other man; He is not the divine Son of God. Relative to receiving the gift of salvation, some people deny the essentiality of baptism in water and teach a faith-only doctrine. Relative to worshipping God, more than a few people say we are not bound to vocal music only; instrumental music is all right too. Relative to living righteous lives, some people say we do not have to "lay aside every weight, and the sin which so easily ensnares us" (Heb. 12:1); God's grace will save us in our sins, they claim.

How do we guard against false doctrine? The same way the church in Galatia did. First, we must preach the true gospel without any additions, subtractions, or substitutions.

Second, we must identify false doctrine and show how it is contrary to the true gospel. Third, we must mark and avoid false teachers. To do less only invites false teachers to introduce a perverted gospel.

FREEDOM IN CHRIST

In Christ we have freedom. While speaking to some believing Jews, Jesus sets forth the following conditional statement: "If ye abide in my word, then are ye truly my disciples" (John 8:31). After identifying His genuine, authentic disciples, Jesus then says, "And ye shall know the truth, and the truth shall make you free" (John 8:32). Combining these statements with verse 34, in which Jesus speaks about being a slave of sin, it is clear the truth has the power to set one free from the shackles of sin. Also, according to Paul in Romans, when an individual obeys the gospel, he is set free from sin and becomes a slave of righteousness (Rom. 6:17-18). Upon being baptized for the remission of sins, a person is "freed from sin as a slave is freed from his master by emancipation" (Lard, 214). Being emancipated from the slavery of sin, a person is free like...when the bird is free to use its wings and to fly, the flower to expand its petals and bloom. We are free to obey our Creator and our Savior in newness of life (Lenski, 428).

Turning to the church in Galatia, Paul contrasts a Christian's freedom in Christ to a yoke of bondage. He writes: "For freedom did Christ set us free: stand fast therefore, and be not entangled again in a yoke of bondage" (Gal. 5:1). The Galatians are given a choice. They can choose to enjoy freedom in Christ or they can decide to go back under a yoke of bondage. Therefore, to comprehend fully the freedom Christians have, one needs to understand what Paul refers to when he uses the term "yoke of bondage" in connection with the Old Testament law.

Earlier in the Galatian letter, Paul has said, "For as many as are of the works of the law are under a curse: for it is written, Cursed is every one who continueth not in all things that are written in the book of the law, to do them" (Gal. 3:10). The word "curse" signifies the condemnation and punishment that comes upon a person who has sinned.

Ezekiel has spoken pointedly of this curse when he tells us the penalty of sin is spiritual death (Ezek. 18:20). Sin separates an individual from God, severing fellowship with Him (Isa. 59:1-2). Similarly, the Apostle Paul states clearly sin results in spiritual death, for he says, "For the wages of sin is death; but the free gift of God is eternal life in Christ Jesus our Lord" (Rom. 6:23).

Furthermore, the Old Testament law does not provide an ultimate remedy for the condemnation and punishment resulting from sin. While Paul states in Galatians 3:11 that no person can be right with God by means of the law of Moses, he speaks even more candidly of the law's deficiency at the beginning of Romans 8. Paul says:

There is therefore now no condemnation to them that are in Christ Jesus. For the law of the Spirit of life in Christ Jesus made me free from the law of sin and of death. For what the law could not do, in that it was weak through the flesh, God, sending his own Son in the likeness of sinful flesh and for sin, condemned sin in the flesh: that the ordinance of the law might be fulfilled in us, who walk not after the flesh, but after the Spirit (Rom. 8:1-4).

What is it the Old Testament law cannot do? It cannot make anyone free from the law of sin and death. Obviously, the death referred to in this passage cannot be physical death; for through the years faithful Christians, who were set free from the penalty of sin, have died physically. The term "death" therefore, refers to spiritual death.

In the previous chapter, the apostle mentions the law of sin (Rom. 7:23). This law of sin is the inclination of the flesh to struggle against the law of God and to give in at times to sinful activity. Paul points out the Old Testament law does not have a remedy to the problem of spiritual death caused by sin. Since the curse of the law is spiritual death, and since the law provides no permanent solution for this problem, it is a yoke of bondage. The freedom we have in Christ Jesus is emancipation from this yoke.

Along with being set free from the yoke of bondage, a Christian is unchained from the practice of sin. When a disciple of Christ keeps the commandments of the Lord Jesus, and when he follows His example by walking in His steps, that disciple walks in the light.

Paul says Christians are to walk in newness of life after arising from the waters of baptism (Rom. 6:3-4). Later in this chapter, the apostle says Christians have been set free from being slaves to sin and have become the servants of righteousness (Rom. 6:17-18). God's Word is truth (John 17:17); and the disciple who walks in the truth of God's Word no longer walks in sin. He walks in righteousness. He is not a slave to sin any longer. He has been set free. Moreover, freedom in Christ meant an individual Christian is free to become a useful vessel in the Master's service. The Apostle Paul has written the following:

Now in a great house there are not only vessels of gold and of silver, but also of wood and of earth; and some unto honor, and some unto dishonor. If a man therefore purge himself from these, he shall be a vessel unto honor, sanctified, meet for the master's use, prepared unto every good work. But flee youthful lusts, and follow after righteousness, faith, love, peace, with them that call on the Lord out of a pure heart (2 Tim. 2:20-22).

By being set free from the practice of sin, a Christian becomes a vessel for honor, prepared for good work in the kingdom. It is the obligation of every Christian to keep himself free from sin; that is, to practice the truth and never again to walk in darkness. A Christian has been liberated from slavery to sin and must never turn back. By remaining a servant of righteousness, he remains qualified for devoted service in the kingdom. He is free to be used by the Lord.

LIMITATIONS TO OUR FREEDOM IN CHRIST

Because there is confusion over a Christian's freedom in Christ, it should prove profitable to examine what this freedom does not mean. First, freedom in Christ cannot mean Christians are free from any responsibility to Divine law. According to Matthew's account of the Great Commission (Matt. 28:18-20), Jesus tells His apostles to go and make disciples in every nation. To accomplish the goal of making disciples, they are to do two things: (1) immerse them in water into the name of the Father, the Son, and the Holy Spirit, and (2) teach them to observe all things Jesus has commanded.

From the requirement given the apostles to instruct baptized believers to obey all the commandments the Lord Jesus Christ has set forth, we may accurately infer Christians are subject to the law of Christ. Jesus always speaks the truth. He says we are to keep His commandments. Isn't submission to the Lordship of Jesus Christ and obedience to His commandments a necessary characteristic of a faithful disciple?

After Judas leaves the upper room where Jesus is meeting with His chosen apostles on Thursday evening only hours before His crucifixion, Jesus continues to speak with them about many things. In John 14:15, Jesus says, "If ye love me, ye will keep my commandments." Concerning this verse, William Barclay makes the following observation:

To John, there is only one test of love, and that is obedience. It was by His obedience that Jesus showed His love of God; and it is by our obedience that we must show our love of Jesus (Barclay, 193). To the aforementioned observation, let's add the remarks of brother David Lipscomb:

> If they loved Him as their Lord and Master, they would cherish and obey His commandments. This is the divine test of love. Love as God views it is practical and embodies the actions of the whole man. And the test and proof of love is the desire to do the will and seek the honor of the one whom we love (Lipscomb, 226).

While love for Jesus Christ and obedience to His commandments are not exactly the same thing, Jesus makes it perfectly clear we manifest our love for Him by keeping His commandments. Without obedience to His command-ments, Jesus says one does not really love Him. A person's love for Jesus, we conclude, cannot be sincere and genuine apart from his submissive obedience to the commandments of the Lord Jesus Christ. Love does not set us free from divine law.

In 1 Corinthians 9:21, the Apostle Paul writes this: "...to them that are without law, as without law, not being without law to God, but under law to Christ, that I might gain them that are without law." In the context where this verse appears, Paul is pointing out his flexibility with respect to his missionary methods.

When he goes among Gentiles, he does not insist on following the customs of the law of Moses, especially the rules and regulations pertaining to what foods should be eaten and how it is to be prepared. When he is among the Gentiles, he accommodates himself to their customs and ways, so long as these customs do not go against the law of Christ. Clearly, Paul considers himself to be under law to Christ. In regard to matters of indifference, the apostle is flexible and accommodating. With respect to the requirements of the Lord Jesus, however, he humbly submits in faithful obedience. He understands he is amenable to the law of Christ. He knows his freedom in Christ does not mean he is set free from divine law.

Second, freedom in Christ cannot mean Christians are free from any responsibility to minister to others. On Thursday evening prior to His crucifixion on Friday, Jesus washes the feet of the apostles (John 13:1-11). After Jesus washes their feet, He sits down and says the following:

Ye call me, Teacher, and, Lord: and ye say well; for so I am. If I then, the Lord and the Teacher, have washed your feet, ye also ought to wash one another's feet. For I have given you an example, that ye also should do as I have done to you. Verily, verily, I say unto you, a servant is not greater than his lord; neither one that is sent greater than he that sent him. If ye know these things, blessed are ye if ye do them (John 13:13-17).

Jesus says He has given them an example which they are to follow. Even though He is the Lord of all, Jesus performs the service of a lowly slave, whose job is to wash the feet of those who enter a house. He has humbly washed the feet of His apostles. However, this example has to do with more than merely washing feet; for in this act of humble service, Jesus sets forth a great principle. True greatness is to be found only in humble service to others, not in positions of prestige or power. Since a servant is not greater than his Lord, and since the Lord has given an example of humble service, a faithful servant will walk in the steps of his Master and will seek to minister to the needs of others. Freedom in Christ does not set us free from humble service to others.

Furthermore, Jesus emphasizes humble service to others by what He says in Matthew 25:31-46. In this passage, Jesus speaks about what will happen when He comes again with all the angels. His coming will be a time of separation. He tells how the sheep will be placed on His right hand and the goats will be placed on His left hand. To the sheep He will say, "Come, ye blessed of my Father, inherit the kingdom prepared for you from the foundation of the world" (Matt. 25:34). To the goats He will say, "Depart from me, ye cursed, into the eternal fire which is prepared for the devil and his angels" (Matt. 25:41). The sheep will go to heaven. The goats will be cast into hell.

By what criterion will Jesus determine who are sheep or who are goats? Jesus said He will separate the sheep from the goats on the basis of how an individual reacted to human need. Those who feed the hungry, give a drink to the thirsty, minister to the sick, etc., will inherit heaven as his eternal home. Those who do not do these things will be punished in the eternal fires of hell. Jesus places upon us the divine responsibility to help those in need. Therefore, freedom in Christ cannot mean we are set free from humble service to others.

A word of caution is in order at this point. Jesus is not saying a person can go to heaven without obeying the gospel. To say a person can go to heaven only on the basis of his having helped others in the hour of their need is to say something that is not true. Numerous passages speak of the essentiality of faith, repentance, baptism, and faithful obedience to all Jesus has commanded. The point of this passage is to make it perfectly clear, if we fail to minister to others in keeping with our abilities and opportunities, we will not be allowed to enjoy heaven in eternity. We have freedom in Christ, and we are required to minister to others. Both things are equally true.

Third, freedom in Christ cannot mean Christians are set free from having to appear before the Lord on the Day of Judgment. Romans 14 deals with things which are indifferent in themselves; that is, they do not have anything to do with either the sin of omission or the sin of commission.

For example, they could eat meat or not eat meat without sinning. Eating meat is a matter of indifference; however, when one is fully persuaded in his heart that eating meat is a sin, it is a sin to him (Rom. 14:22-23). A person who holds to such scruples is labeled as "one who is weak in the faith," one who does not have a correct biblical understanding. In regard to such matters, the weak brothers are not to judge the strong, and the strong brothers are not to despise the weak; for both, says Paul, will stand before the judgment seat of Christ (Rom. 14:10). The fact they will stand before the Lord Jesus Christ to be judged means they ought not to judge one another regarding matters of indifference. In verse twelve, Paul says, "So then each one of us shall give account of himself to God." Commenting on this verse, Moses E. Lard wrote the following:

> As each of us will have to account to God for his conduct, and be judged accordingly, it is idle to be judging and despising one another here. Our judgments are not final, nor will any one either stand or fall by them (Lard, 421).

It must be kept in mind that Paul's injunction against judging has to be confined to such matters as were under consideration; that is, matters of indifference. Keeping these things in mind, we also are to understand each Christian will have to give an account of his life's work before the judgment seat of Christ. Christians will be held responsible for their stewardship; for it is indeed certain they will appear before the Lord Jesus Christ on the Day of Judgment. We are not free from accountability. We will be held responsible regarding how well we carried out our duties. To the brethren in Corinth, Paul says the following:

> Wherefore also we make it our aim, whether at home or absent, to be well-pleasing unto him. For we must all be made manifest before the judgment-seat of Christ; that each one may receive the things done in the body, according to what he hath done, whether it be good or bad (2 Cor. 5:9-10).

Paul affirms he has one over-arching goal. His aim is to live in the manner which is always pleasing to God. He adds, moreover, this is his goal here upon the earth, and it will even be his goal in the world to come. Paul lives to serve God, not himself or other men.

As an aid to help him achieve his aim, Paul lives each day in the awareness that he is accountable to God. He knows the day will come when he will given an answer for how he has handled his stewardship. Paul understands we all will stand before Christ one day. Paul says we will be judged according to our works. Along with all others, Christians will face the Lord in judgment one day. Therefore, freedom in Christ does not mean we are set free from an appearance before the Lord on that day.

CONCLUSION

The church in Galatia teaches many important lessons. Among them we are reminded how soon false doctrine may be embraced and how to avoid a departure from the true gospel. In addition, we learn the meaning of our liberty in Christ. Especially, we see the freedom in which "Christ set us free" does not mean we are freed from any responsibility to Divine law, from any responsibility to minister to others, or from having to appear before the Lord on the Day of Judgment. Our challenge is to live our lives in keeping with these important lessons.

STUDY QUESTIONS

1. What is the constant danger facing the church?
2. How does the church in Galatia illustrate this danger?
3. What is the sure safeguard that protects the church from the danger it constantly faces?
4. In what ways so some today fail to maintain the integrity of the gospel?
5. What all does the "curse" signify in Galatians 3:10?
6. What could the Old Testament law never do?
7. From what two things are Christians not set free?
8. How do John 14:15 and 1 Corinthians 9:21 show Christians are responsible to obey the law of Christ?
9. What scriptural considerations show we are responsible to minister to others?
10. What did Paul tell the Corinthians about the judgment seat of Christ?

WORKS CITED

All Bible quotations are taken from the American Standard Version unless otherwise indicated.

Barclay, William. The Gospel of John: Volume 2. Louisville, KY: Westminster John Knox Press, 2001.

Lard, Moses E. A Commentary on Paul's Letter to Romans. 1875. Delight AR: Gospel Light Publishing Company.

Lenski, R. C. H. Interpretation of St. Paul's Epistles to the Galatians, to the Ephesians, to the Philippians. Peabody, MA: Hendrickson Publishers, 2001.

Interpretation of St. Paul's Epistle to the Romans. Peabody, MA: Hendrickson Publishers, 2001.

Lipscomb, David. A Commentary on the Gospel of John. Nashville, TN: Gospel Advocate Company, 1966.

The Church at Jerusalem

INTRODUCTION

Some of the most popular websites for people to visit today are websites dealing with family history or heritage. Many websites can help someone trace their family history. Most who visit these websites want to know about their roots. They are curious about who their ancestors were, what they did, and what intriguing information they may be able to find in their family history. Looking at our past can help us to identify just who we are, or at least, who we are supposed to be. The church is no different. Looking at the beginning of the church can help us understand who we are, or who we are supposed to be.

What a wonderful study it is to look at the churches of the first century. So much can be learned about what God expects of us and who He wants us to be by looking at the body of Christ located throughout those regions we read about in the New Testament times. Studying the past is certainly a learning tool. Paul said in Romans 15:4 the things which were written before time were written for "our learning". Although this refers to the Old Testament, the same is true of the New Testament. It contains not only lessons to learn, but God's will for us in our lives today. What better way to understand how we are to conduct ourselves as the New Testament church in today's time than to go back and look at the models God provided for us. In this study we will look at the very first church that came into existence, the church in Jerusalem.

BEGINNING OF THE CHURCH IN JERUSALEM

The children of Israel had been looking forward to the coming of Christ and the establishing of His kingdom. Although they mistook His kingdom for an earthly one, everything in the Old Testament was pointing toward Christ's coming and His kingdom. His kingdom that was spoken of was the Church. Isaiah prophesied about the Church coming in Isaiah 2:2-3,

And it shall come to pass in the last days, that the mountain of the Lord's house shall be established in the top of the mountains, and shall be exalted above the hills; and all nations shall flow unto it. And many people shall go and say, 'Come ye, and let us go up to the mountain of the Lord, to the house of the God of Jacob; and He will teach us of His ways, and we will walk in His paths.' For out of Zion shall go forth the law, and the word of the Lord from Jerusalem.

Isaiah's prophecy was that the kingdom, or church, would begin in Jerusalem. Christ himself made several statements the church would begin in Jerusalem. In Luke 24:47 He said, "... repentance and remission of sins should be preached in His name among all nations, beginning at Jerusalem." Later in verse 49 of the same chapter, Christ told them to tarry in the city of Jerusalem until they were endued with power from on high. In Mark 9:1, Jesus said to those present that day, "Verily I say unto you, that there be some of them that stand here, which shall not taste of death, till they have seen the kingdom of God come with power." Obviously Christ was referring to the same coming of His kingdom. It was a kingdom that would come during the lifetime of some of those present. We also see from these prophecies it was a kingdom that would come with power. These prophecies by Christ were pointing toward the coming of His church in Jerusalem. When did we see this church come?

In Acts 1:8 Christ spoke face to face with His apostles one last time before He ascended back into Heaven. They had been commanded by Him in verse 4 not to depart from Jerusalem, but to wait for the promise of the Father. In verse 8, he tells them they would first receive power, and after that, the Holy Ghost would come upon them.

In chapter 2 of Acts, we see this exact thing happening to them in the city of Jerusalem. In verses 2-4 they received the power and then the Holy Ghost. From there Peter spoke to the multitude of people that had gathered from throughout the area. He preached to them Christ; the Bible tells us the church began that day in Jerusalem.

The beginning of the church in Jerusalem also teaches us about the admission standards God has set forth for His church. As Peter convicted those that day that Christ was the Son of God, those who believed wanted to know what needed to be done (Acts 2:37). Peter's reply to them was to "repent, and be baptized every one of you in the name of Jesus Christ for the remission of sins" (Acts 2:38). Later in verse 41 the Bible further explains all who gladly received the Word were baptized, and the number added was about 3,000 souls. But what were they added to? In verse 47 the Bible explains, "And the Lord added to the church daily such as should be saved." It is clear those who received the Word (believed) and were baptized were added to the church. This matches exactly what Jesus had said would be the admission standards in Mark 16:16. Those who were added in Acts 2 were a part of this first congregation of the Lord's church in Jerusalem. This was the first and original location of the body of Christ.

SPIRIT OF THE CHURCH IN JERUSALEM

One way many churches need to look to the first church for guidance is in the very spirit of the church. The church in Jerusalem certainly portrayed many great qualities congregations everywhere should seek to emulate. When you read the first few chapters of Acts, you cannot help but notice what a close knit group they had become. They truly understood what it meant to be brothers and sisters in Christ. In fact, if we were to sum up in just one word the attitude and spirit of the church in Jerusalem, that one word could easily be "unity". Let us examine from the scriptures the attitude of the church in Jerusalem.

The church in Jerusalem was an abiding church. Here we see a congregation of people that continued or abided in God's word and His work. In Acts 2:42 it says, "And they continued steadfastly in the apostles' doctrine and fellowship, and in breaking of bread, and in prayers." Jesus Himself said, "If ye continue in My word, then are ye My disciples indeed" (John 8:31). It is important that we continue in the doctrine of God's Word. It is the truth of His Word that will set us free (John 8:32) and will save us (Rom. 1:16). Paul even stated if anyone, even an angel from heaven, taught anything different than the gospel, let him be accursed (Gal. 1:6-9). This idea of abiding, or continuing, in the doctrine is taught throughout the scriptures.

We also see a congregation of people that continued in fellowship together. Certainly God created fellowship to be something special among His people. Fellowship with other Christians is not just merely for our recreation or to pass time. God intended it for a very important purpose. Hebrews 3:13 says we should "exhort one another daily, while it is called 'Today,' lest any of you be hardened through the deceitfulness of sin." We need to encourage one another because of the many trials and troubles we face in this life. We also need encouragement for ourselves so we do not give up or lose heart. Hebrews 10:24-25 tells us of the importance of not forsaking the assembling of ourselves together. It says we should "consider one another in order to stir up love and good works, not forsaking the assembling of ourselves together, as is the manner of some, but exhorting one another". We receive benefits in being in fellowship with our fellow Christians. In fact, as we will continue to see, their fellowship brought them closer together than some earthly families are today. This enabled them to withstand persecution and those things which might pull them away from the cause of Christ.

The church in Jerusalem was also a very prayerful church. Verse 42 says they continued steadfastly in prayer. We are told to "pray without ceasing" (1 Thess. 5:17) as well as to "pray for one another" (James 5:16). The effectual fervent prayer of a righteous man availeth much (James 5:16). Certainly we can have an impact on others through our offering of prayers on their behalf.

An example of this is found in Acts 12 beginning in verse 5. When Peter found himself in prison, the Bible says, "but constant prayer was offered to God for him by the church." It goes on to tell us their prayers as a congregation were answered. We should follow the example of the church in Jerusalem by being a prayerful church and praying for those in need.

We also find the church in Jerusalem was a very giving and generous congregation. In fact, there is a certain spirit we see in this congregation that almost has ceased to exist in today's churches. Here we see what we could call sacrificial giving. How many people today in the Lord's church would be willing to sacrifice or give something up just to give to someone in need? We see this sacrificial spirit in verses 44 and 45 of Acts 2. It first speaks to the fact they had all things in common. In others words, there was no "mine" and "yours", only "ours". What belonged to one person belonged to them all. Verse 45 says they went so far as to sell their possessions and goods and divide them among all to give to those who had need. This spirit is seen to continue in Acts 4:32-37. Verse 34 says not one of them lacked because they distributed to each as anyone had need. What a wonderful spirit those in the church in Jerusalem had! Certainly if we want to be more like the first century church, we need to be a more giving and sharing congregation.

This was a unified congregation of the Lord's people as well. Acts 2:46 says they continued daily with "one accord". This phrase "one accord" means unanimously, with one mind. They were all of the same mindset. Paul challenges us to have the mind of Christ, and in that way we too can be unified (Phil. 2:5-11). Acts 4:32 says they were of "one heart and one soul". We have already seen they were unified in their giving, in prayer, in fellowship, and in doctrine. When a group of the Lord's children are unified and work together, much can be accomplished together. This principle is seen in the Old Testament account of the Tower of Babel in Genesis 11:1-9. The Lord recognized when people worked together "nothing will be restrained from them, which they have imagined to do" (Gen. 11:6). That certainly is true in light of Philippians 4:13 if we are working together for the Lord!

The church in Jerusalem was a happy and thankful congregation as well. This was a church that recognized their blessings from God and was thankful even for the most basic things of life. Acts 2:46 teaches us they ate their meat with gladness and singleness of heart. Another word for singleness there is simplicity. It is easy to take things for granted, especially the most basic blessings from God. When we are thankful, we are certainly happier and cheerful in this life. Paul taught we should even come to God in prayer with thanksgiving each time we let our requests be made known to Him (Phil. 4:6). Certainly we need to recognize the source of all of our blessings (James 1:17; Matt. 6:11). As Americans today, it is difficult for us at times to have that same singleness or simplicity of heart. We worry and stress over many things that really are not important in the grand scheme of things. Often in foreign countries you can see this attitude more prevalent among the people who obey God's word. Certainly we will be more blessed when we release the worries of this world and concentrate on God's work.

One more characteristic we see of the church in Jerusalem is it was a respected church in the community. Acts 2:47 says they had "favor with all the people". This does not mean everyone agreed with them. Certainly there were those who were in disagreement on their religious stance in Jesus Christ. However, they were conducting themselves in such a way that brought respect to the name of Christ. They certainly were very zealous for the cause of Christ, but also careful to live in a way that would be pleasing to Christ and not bring shame or reproach upon His holy name.

GROWTH OF THE CHURCH IN JERUSALEM

The church in Jerusalem certainly started out with a "bang". On the day of Pentecost, the Bible records "about 3,000 souls" were added to the church. What a wonderful start to the Lord's church on that day! However, the growth did not stop there. The Bible says in Acts 2:47, "And the Lord added to the church daily such as should be saved."

There was no sporadic growth of this church in the first century; it was a growth that was taking place on a "daily" basis. Acts 4:4 tells us the number of them who obeyed came to be about 5,000. Approximately an additional 2,000 were added to their numbers. Acts 5:14 says "believers were the more added to the Lord, multitudes both of men and women". Again in Acts 6:7, "And the word of God increased; and the number of the disciples multiplied in Jerusalem greatly". Certainly great things were happening for the church in Jerusalem. This congregation was growing at an astronomical rate. This certainly teaches us the power the church had in the first century.

How did they get those types of results? Is it possible for today's church to grow at such a rate? Many congregations today spend a lot of money, time, and energy using different methods to try and "grow the church". We have church growth workshops, seminars, gospel meetings, and the like. While there is nothing wrong with any of these things, it certainly would help us to look at how the church in Jerusalem was able to grow as it did in the first century. There were no "special worship services" designed to draw in crowds. Very simply the Word of God was being taught, and it was the Word of God that was causing people to want to become New Testament Christians.

Acts 2:46 tells us they were continuing daily with one accord in the temple. Obviously, teaching was going on there as well. In fact, verse 42 says they continued in the apostles' doctrine. Part of that doctrine would have been found in Matthew 28:19-20 where Jesus commanded all be taught the gospel and to observe all He had commanded. The growth of the first century church was due largely to the fact that everyone bore the responsibility to go and teach on a daily basis. It was not just the job of the "preacher" or the "elders" but rather the job of every child of God. Acts 8:4 speaks of those who were scattered going everywhere and preaching the Word. Romans 1:16 says the gospel of Christ is the power of God unto salvation. That is what convicts men and will bring them to salvation (Heb. 4:12), not a "special worship service" or an entertaining show.

Those in the church in Jerusalem believed in the power of God's Word and went out every day to spread this message to those who were lost. Is it possible for us today to add 3,000 to the body in one service? It is probably not likely we would see those kinds of numbers here in America. However, we can certainly grow if we will go every day and take the responsibility as members of His body to teach those who are lost. If the growth of the Lord's church is not seen today, it is because we are not diligent in our responsibility to spread His message to all.

STRUCTURE OF THE CHURCH IN JERUSALEM

The book of Acts also reveals to us the structure of the church in Jerusalem. In Acts 6, a complaint had arisen against the Hebrews by the Hellenists. This was due to the fact the Hellenists' widows were being neglected in the daily distributions, so this was not a church without problems or issues. To correct this, the apostles told the congregation to seek out some men that would serve as deacons or servants. These were to be men of good reputation, full of the Holy Spirit and wisdom. These men were able to do some of the work of the church so the apostles could continue in their prayer and ministry of the Word and spreading the gospel. This church also had elders to shepherd the flock as well. In Acts 15, we see the congregation in Jerusalem had elders. These elders met with the apostles in this particular account to discuss a matter. However, we can see the makeup of this church leadership contained both elders and deacons.

PERSECUTION AGAINST THE CHURCH IN JERUSALEM

Jesus had warned His disciples there would be persecution they would have to face or endure if they would be His followers. In John 15:20, Jesus warned if they had persecuted Him, they would certainly persecute any who would follow Him as well. This certainly took place with those in the church in Jerusalem.

In fact, the first Christian martyr was a man by the name of Stephen, who was a deacon at the church in Jerusalem. Acts 7 first records this persecution that happened to Stephen. It was apparent many Jews were not happy with what was being preached concerning Christ as being the Son of God and the accusations against them. After Stephen preached straightforward to them, they became angry and cast him out of the city and stoned him to death. Saul was present and consented to the death of Stephen (Acts 7:58). We see this same Saul was one who was a main persecutor of the church in Jerusalem. In Acts 9:13 we see Ananias' concern over Saul when he said to the Lord "I have heard by many of this man, how much evil he hath done to Thy saints at Jerusalem." In Acts 8:1 the Bible records, "And Saul was consenting unto his death. And at that time there was a great persecution against the church which was at Jerusalem; and they were all scattered abroad throughout the regions of Judea and Samaria, except the apostles." Verse 4 of the same chapter tells us, "Therefore they that were scattered abroad went everywhere preaching the word." Some very intense persecution took place upon those in the church in Jerusalem. Many of them were scattered throughout the regions of Judea and Samaria. No doubt, this caused the numbers at the church in Jerusalem to dwindle. However, those who were scattered continued to preach the gospel everywhere they went. This persecution of the church seemed to work out for the best. It might remind us of a quote spoken by Joseph in Genesis 50:20, "But as for you, ye thought evil against me; but God meant it unto good". God was able to use this persecution to have His Word spread throughout other regions, so many might hear the gospel and have opportunity to be saved. The Jews did not cease there with the persecution however. Later in the book of Acts, we see where those in Jerusalem wanted to have Paul killed because of his stance for Christ and the gospel. Paul declared himself ready to die at Jerusalem for the name of the Lord Jesus (Acts 21:13). In Acts 23, some of the Jews banded together and made an oath they would neither eat nor drink until they had killed Paul. Certainly this was no light persecution that had come upon those Christians in Jerusalem. It was obvious they would not only preach and teach Christ, but would be followers of Him as well.

CONCLUSION

The church in Jerusalem was certainly a model church for many reasons. The enthusiasm and unity of these brethren is something that should be taught to Christians everywhere. This congregation began in the exact place that prophets of old had prophesied. It came with power and grew by leaps and bounds. It did undergo some very intense persecutions but managed to stay faithful in the work of the Lord. Those who were scattered took what they had learned in Jerusalem and spread God's message and His work in other areas that needed it badly. May we always seek to learn from this first century church exactly who we are and what God wants us to be in this world. May we be as unified in doing the will of God as these Christians were in Jerusalem nearly 2,000 years ago.

STUDY QUESTIONS

1. What Old Testament prophet prophesied the church would be established in Jerusalem?
2. What 2 things did the apostles receive in Acts 2 that had been told to them by Christ in Acts 1?
3. What were the admission standards God set forth for His church we read about in Acts 2?
4. What is one word that could be used to sum up or describe the spirit of the church in Jerusalem from Acts 2 - 4?
5. Name 3 characteristics we read about in Acts 2 and following concerning the church in Jerusalem.
6. How was the church in Jerusalem able to grow as it did in the first century?
7. What was the structure of the church in Jerusalem like?
8. Who was the first Christian martyr we read about in Acts from the church in Jerusalem and what work had he been appointed to?
9. Who was one of the main persecutors of the church in Jerusalem?
10. What did those who were persecuted do after they were scattered?

The Church at Laodicea

The Churches OF THE New Testament

INTRODUCTION

The church in Laodicea, when first planted, was "on fire" for the Lord; now, they made Him sick! They were on the verge of suffering a most fatal experience, that of being vomited out of His mouth because of their lukewarmness. They had now become the epitome of apathy and compromise. What had brought about such a drastic change? How did Christ address this distressing problem?

Christ in His Revelation to the apostle John addressed seven churches in Asia Minor. Inasmuch as there were more than seven congregations in Asia, the number "seven" [which means completeness] implies that the Lord's letters spoke not only to all of His churches in the territory but also to all congregations at any time or place—including those of our day. Inasmuch as those churches possessed the same qualities present in congregations today, the Lord's messages to those seven churches are more up-to-date than the morning newspaper; any church can see itself mirrored in Christ's letters to the churches of Asia (Rev. 2, 3).

In His letters to the churches, the Lord addressed their spiritual conditions and commended and/or condemned them, depending upon those conditions. What He required of those churches was based upon His absolute standard for His church. Only the church in Laodicea had nothing about it which he could commend; Smyrna and Philadelphia had nothing to condemn. Ephesus, Pergamum, Thyatira, and Sardis had both commendable and condemnable characteristics. Each of the churches was urged, "He that hath an ear, let him hear what the Spirit saith to the churches."

With every warning of punishment for sin [here as elsewhere in the Scriptures], there is an accompanying offer of mercy, if the people/congregations will repent. God does not "wish for any to perish" (2 Pet. 3:9); thus, in this last of the letters to the seven churches, the loving Redeemer is pictured on the outside of the congregation at Laodicea, gently knocking at the door of their hearts and pleading for entrance (Rev. 3:14-22).

In examining the church of Laodicea, let us notice the following six points suggested by the Lord's letter: the city of Laodicea, the history of the church, the identity of the writer, the condition of the congregation, the Lord's plea, and the Lord's assurances.

THE CITY OF LAODICEA, LOCATION OF THE CHURCH

Inasmuch as several cities were called by the same name, this Laodicea was distinguished from the others by adding the identifying phrase "on the Lycus," about one and one-half mile in distance. The Lycus River was a tributary of the Maeander, from which the winding river gave us the English word "meander." Located on the border of the provinces of Phrygia and Caria [Asia], Laodicea was some ninety miles east of Ephesus and forty miles southeast of Philadelphia. Also in the Lycus valley, Colosse was some ten miles to the east and Hierapolis six miles to the north of Laodicea. The city served as the capital of Phrygia, thus a city of note at the time of the New Testament.

Earlier called Diospolis [named after its "tutelary" ("watching over") god Zeus, who was the supreme deity of the ancient Greeks and identified with the Roman "Jupiter"] and later Rhoas, the city was subject to violent earthquakes. The city was rebuilt likely in the same location by the Seleucid [Syrian] king Antiochus II Theos (261-246 B.C.), who named it after his wife Laodice [who later poisoned him].

A modest city at first, Asia would soon become a province of Rome [190 B.C.], and Laodicea would grow in prominence and become wealthy. Earlier enamored by Grecian culture and idolatry, it would eventually be captivated by and become a center for emperor worship. Laodicea was in a strategic location;

it was on the major Roman road which led from Ephesus across Asia Minor into the interior to Antioch of Syria. Much commerce took place on this route; thus, Laodicea greatly prospered financially and became a center of finance and banking.

A number of local industries also contributed to its wealth. One, they were known for producing very popular, high quality, warm, soft clothing from a shiny, black wool of the area's particular breed of sheep. Two, they were broadly recognized for their medical school, which specialized in eye treatment. Having developed a special soothing liniment for the eyes [Phrygian powder], the treatment in tablet form was widely used in the Roman world. The city would have a natural attraction for many peoples, including the Jews and those who were wealthy retirees. On one occasion when destroyed by an earthquake, the city did not call upon Rome but rebuilt it with their own wealth.

Lacking a supply of fresh, cold water, Laodicea received its water by aqueduct from a hot spring, which rendered it lukewarm by the time it mixed with cooler water and reached the city. In view of the above-mentioned facts concerning the city, it is appropriate to quote William M. Ramsay, scholarly archaeologist and expert on early church history:

There is no city whose spirit and nature are more difficult to describe than Laodicea. There are no extremes, and hardly any very strongly marked features. But in this even balance lies its peculiar character. Those were the qualities that contributed to make it essentially the successful trading city, the city of bankers and finance, which could adapt itself to the needs and wishes of others, ever pliable and accommodating, full of the spirit of compromise.

The Laodicean Church is neither one thing nor another. It is given to compromise. It cannot thoroughly reject the temptations and allurements of the world. And therefore it shall be rejected absolutely, and inexorably by Him whose faithfulness and truth reject all half-heartedness and compromise (The Letters to the Seven Churches of Asia, Baker Book House, 1979, pp. 422-423, 424).

THE HISTORY OF THE CHURCH

The time and details of the planting of the Lord's church in Laodicea are unknown. It could have been started by Jewish Christians who moved to the city. We do know that when Paul taught in the school of Tyrannus for two years, Luke records that the result was that "all they that dwelt in Asia heard the word of the Lord, both Jews and Greeks" (Acts 19:10).

Inasmuch as three churches located in the Lycus valley [Colossae, Hierapolis, and Laodicea] were mentioned by Paul in his letter to the Colossians, the congregation at Laodicea had to have been started before Paul wrote the letter in about 60 A.D. from prison. His writings in Colossians must have been pertinent to the Laodicean congregation relative to Gnosticism, et al., because Paul's instruction was that the epistle to Colossae was "to be read also in the church of the Laodiceans; and that ye also read the epistle from Laodicea" (Col. 4:16).

Paul dearly loved the church at Laodicea, as shown in his Colossians letter; he had worked hard for them. "For I would have you know how greatly I strive for you, and for them at Laodicea, and for as many as have not seen my face in the flesh..." (2:3). Some hold that this means he had not seen them personally; however, it seems to this writer the opposite is true--that Paul is stating that he had a deep care not only for those like the Colossians and Laodiceans whom he had seen but also for other dear brethren whom he had not seen.

As to the origin of the churches in the Lycus valley, the Scriptures state that Paul and Silas preached in Phrygia (Acts 15:40-41; 16:1-6). Did they preach personally in the valley? Would they preach in the principle Phrygian cities of Colossae and Laodicea, which was the capital? To say the least, Paul certainly knew their first teachers and that they had been taught "the grace of God in truth" (Col. 1:3-8; cf. 2:6-7). Epaphras had kept Paul abreast of the situation in Colossae and Laodicea (1:7-8), and he was one of the Colossians (4:12-13); however, he is not identified as having begun the work there. Thus, Paul personally may have carried the gospel to the valley (1:21-25).

Paul wrote numerous letters which are not preserved for us [they are not needed], which would include [for example] his first and third letters to the Corinthians and his letter to the Laodiceans (4:16).

CHRIST, THE WRITER TO THE CHURCH

Christ the Lord identified Himself to the Laodicean church thus: "These things saith the A-men, the faithful and true witness, the beginning of the creation of God" (Rev. 3:14). The word "Amen" is here used as a proper name of Christ, the only place it is thus used in the Bible. From the Hebrew, it is used in Isaiah 65:16, "...so that he who blesseth himself in the earth shall bless himself in the God of truth; and he that sweareth in the earth shall swear by the God of truth" ["Heb. Amen," ASV margin]. Its meaning is "to make firm, steadfast, to prop." In Christ, Paul stated, "is the yea: wherefore also through him is the A-men," or the absolute certainty, or truth, of the message (2 Cor. 1:17-21). Often, John records Christ's statements of this word doubled, such as "Verily, verily, I say unto thee, Except one be born of water and the spirit, he cannot enter the kingdom of God"—"truly, truly," for emphasis (John 3:5). What a contrast is Christ's absolute, yet, truthful, dependable, unchanging fidelity to the dreadful lack of such fidelity on the part of the Laodicean church! What a contrast are the true riches in "the truth," Christ (John 14:6), to "the deceitfulness of riches" of this world (Mat. 13:22)!

He also identified Himself as "the faithful and true witness" (cf. Rev. 1:5), meaning that what He states should be believed by children of God. God the Father spoke through Him (Heb. 1:1-3; 2:1-2). Being deity Himself, His testimony is true. Thus, His warnings and admonitions must be heeded. Is He not in the midst of the churches, implying [among other things] intimate knowledge of them (Rev. 1:11-16)?

In addition He identified Himself as "the beginning of the creation of God." Christ, the Alpha and the Omega (1:8; 21:6; 22:13), in the active sense—not passive, is the Source, the Agent through whom all things were created (John 1:1-3, 14).

[Although some attempt to make Christ a created being and thus to do away with His deity, the Bible soundly refutes such infidelity (Col. 1:15-17; John 1:10; et al.). Inasmuch as all created things in heaven, on earth, under the earth, and on the sea praised the Lamb (Rev. 5:13), for He is deity—equal to God the Father, it is unreasonable to hold He is a created being, and yet co-equal and co-eternal with the Father. Since Christ created all things, did He create Himself? Did He give all dominion and glory to Himself and bow down to Himself?]

Because Christ is the Source, the Creator of financial prosperity [since the world is His (Psa. 50:10-12) and since "it is he that giveth thee power to get wealth" (Deu. 8:18)], Laodicea should have given thanks and allegiance to God for their material goods, instead of making the created things their gods. Their earlier dedication, loyalty, and praise to God [being "hot" in God's service] were not to continue. They should have taken seriously Paul's admonitions to the Colossians, which letter Laodicea also received (e.g., Col. 1:12-17).

THE CONDITION OF THE CHURCH

No doubt with a broken heart, as with the rebellious Jews in Matthew 23:37, our Lord wrote, "I know thy works, that thou art neither cold nor hot: I would thou wert cold or hot. So because thou art lukewarm, and neither hot nor cold, I will spew thee out of my mouth. Because thou sayest, I am rich, and have gotten riches, and have need of nothing; and knowest not that thou art the wretched one, and miserable and poor and blind and naked" (Rev. 3:15-17). Reminiscent of the lukewarm, tepid water Laodicea received by aqueduct, Christ charged the brethren with being "neither cold nor hot."

Though they had not fully denied and repudiated Christianity and the Savior, they certainly did not possess the zealous fervency and whole-hearted devotion which earlier characterized them. Whereas Christians are on fire for the Lord, they congratulated themselves on their mediocrity, complacency, and apathy.

Has God ever been able to "stomach" half-hearted fence-straddlers: those who are reluctant to choose whom they will serve (Jos. 24:15), or who halt between two opinions (1 Kin. 18:21), or who try to serve two masters (Matt. 6:24), or who try refusing whether to be for or against Christ (12:30), or who seek to be both in Christ and in the world (1 John 2:15-17; Col. 1:13-14)? Christ abhorred such lukewarmness; it made Him sick; He became nauseated; He would spew, or vomit, them out of His mouth. One sees His reaction toward such a sickening attitude in Matthew 21:31: "Verily I say unto you, that the publicans and the harlots go into the kingdom of God before you." Even those who were "cold," who had completely wrecked their lives like the prodigal son (Luke 15:11-24), could be reached and restored more readily than self-conceited, indifferent souls. What a negative influence and hindrance they are to other children of God! What had contributed to the church's lack of zeal? The writer of Proverbs pleaded of God,

> Two things have I asked of thee; Deny me them not before I die: Remove far from me falsehood and lies; Give me neither poverty nor riches; Feed me with the food that is needful for me: Lest I be full, and deny thee, and say, Who is Jehovah? Or lest I be poor, and steal, and use profanely the name of my God (Pro. 30:7-9).

The church of Laodicea had imbibed the attitude of the city; having physical wealth, they began to place their trust in riches rather than in God (cf. Mark 10:25; 1 Tim. 6:17)—thus their foolish attitude that they had "need of nothing" and their being puffed up with pride.

However, the omniscient Christ who knew their works informed them they were spiritually destitute. Blinded by the world and by wealth, they knew not they were "wretched" [to be pitied; without a Savior]; "miserable" [the condition of those without God in this world, and without hope in the hereafter (1 Cor. 15:19)]; "poor" [spiritually destitute, paupers in God's eyes]; "blind" [unable to see one's own desperate state (Rom. 2:19-23; 2 Pet. 1:9)] and "naked" [instead of being spiritually clothed "in holy array" ("Or, in the beauty of holiness," ASV margin, Psa. 110:3), they were openly exposed before God in all their wickedness]. Indeed, they had lost their spiritual vision and zeal; they were "blind, seeing only what is near, having forgotten the cleansing from [their] old sins" (2 Pet. 1:9). Was there any hope?

THE LORD'S INSTRUCTIONS AND INVITATION TO THE CHURCH

Christ Jesus counseled the Laodiceans to amend their ways and return to Him, their only hope. The Psalmist observed, "The sacrifices of God are a broken spirit: A broken and a contrite heart, O God, thou wilt not despise" (Psa. 51:17).

The loving Lord pleaded,
> I counsel thee to buy of me gold refined by fire, that thou mayest become rich; and white garments, that thou mayest clothe thyself, and that the shame of thy nakedness be not made manifest; and eye-salve to anoint thine eyes, that thou mayest see. As many as I love, I reprove and chasten: be zealous therefore, and repent. Behold, I stand at the door and knock: if any man hear my voice and open the door, I will come in to him, and will sup with him, and he with me (Rev. 3:18-20).

The Friend of Sinners is the Source of pure spiritual gold, pure spiritual raiments, and pure spiritual vision; they were to "buy of me"—not trust in themselves, Christ stated. They were destitute but could turn back to Christ for genuine wealth, naked but could seek holy garments by being again cleansed by the blood of Christ (1 John 1:7-10), blind but could be healed of that fatal malady through the wisdom of Christ, to see their sin of indifference (Jam. 1:25). How ironic it was to be spiritually poor in the midst of physical wealth, naked in the midst of physical garments, and blind in the midst of physical eye-salve and the medical center!

Please note they could not be healed by grace alone; they had to heed Christ's counsel and "buy of Him" gold, white [pure] garments and clothe themselves, and anoint their blind eyes. Grace requires an active response. The Savior loves us and therefore rebukes and chastens (Heb. 12:5-11); however, we must be active in being "zealous" and in repentance (Luke 13:1-5).

The Lord was on the outside of their hearts, seeking entrance. But, the door opened from the inside. Even Christ cannot impinge upon man's free will; He will not, He cannot [as the fabled Big Bad Wolf] kick in the door. Whether He could bless them and commune with them in sweet fellowship (1 John 1:3) in the great supper depended upon their receptivity of His loving, impassioned plea (Luke 14:15-24).

THE LORD'S ASSURANCES IF THE CHURCH REPENTS

Envision the Lord's promise of exaltation to the overcomer, to share in His own victory in the church, wherein are all spiritual blessings (Eph. 1:3).

He that overcometh, I will give to him to sit down with me in my throne, as I also overcame, and sat down with my Father in his throne. He that hath an ear, let him hear what the Spirit saith to the churches (Rev. 3:21-22).

Those who share in His sufferings (2 Tim. 2:12) experience the victory over sin in His church/kingdom. Our Lord suffered the death of the cross and is now reigning as King (Acts 2:29-36; Heb. 1:3, 13) on His throne (1:8-9). As Christ overcame and now reigns, Paul told the Ephesians they had been raised from being dead in their trespasses, that Christ "raised us up with him, and made us to sit with him in the heavenly places [the church/kingdom], in Christ Jesus" (Eph. 2:6); thus, we "reign in life through the one, even Jesus Christ" (Rom. 8:17). Peter wrote, "... insomuch as ye are partakers of Christ's sufferings, rejoice; that at the revelation of his glory also ye may rejoice with exceeding joy" (1 Pet. 4:13). The sufferings and glories in the Lord's kingdom here are but a foretaste of the eternal rest and glories of the eternal, glorified kingdom in Heaven at last. "There remaineth therefore a Sabbath rest for the people of God" (Heb. 4:9).

CONCLUSION

At times my Mother would ask me when a child, "Son, don't you have ears?" What victory Christ offers to those who overcome!
"Who is on the Lord's side?" May our answer be, "Master, Here am I."

STUDY QUESTIONS

1. Instead of being on fire for the Lord, they made the Lord what?
2. The number seven means what?
3. The city was subject to violet what?
4. Laodicea was a center of what two things?
5. Laodicea received its water from a hot spring which by the time it got to the people it was what?
6. The word "amen" as used in Revelation 3:14 is a proper name for who?
7. Identifying Himself as "the beginning of the creation of God" was saying that He was what?
8. Does Christ like it when men are lukewarm?
9. They had lost their spiritual what?
10. If we share in His suffering (2 Tim. 2:12) we will experience what over sin?

The Church at Pergamos

The Churches OF THE New Testament

INTRODUCTION

Background of Pergamos

Pergamos was about sixty miles north of Smyrna. The river Caicus ran just to the south of the city, while the river Selinus flowed through it. The city was founded by Philelaerus, who was the lieutenant of King Lysamachus during the wars with Seleucus. The modern name for Pergamos is Bergama, Turkey. We read:

> Pergamum was the famous site of the temple to Aesculapius, the Greek God of healing supposed to be the founder of medical science and immortalized in the sky as the constellation Ophiuchus. The city became the seat of Babylonian sun worship, a noble center of idolatry and demon controlled religions with splendid temples to Nature. People from all over the Roman empire came to seek healing in this pagan temple and the shrine area was inhabited by thousands of harmless snakes. On the hills of Acropolis stood resplendent buildings, statuary, palaces and the great library as well as the temples and an altar of "Zeus the Savior." Medicine and science was worshipped here and the symbol of their worship was the serpent. The snake was carried down into our own day with a staff entwined with serpents called the caduceus, still using the snake as a symbol for the medical arts; Aesculapius is depicted holding the caduceus in his hand.[1]

The same writer continues:
> Pergamum became the chief town of the new province of Asia, and the site of the first temple of the Caesar cult, dedicated to the goddess Roma and the emperor Augustus in 29 BC. Pergamum, since 29 BC, had been active in the promotion of the imperial religion and became the provincial center of the Roman state religion. With this emphasis it was but natural that the Christians of Pergamum should undergo persecution for refusing to worship the emperor.2

These historical notes help us better understand some of the problems besetting the Christians in Pergamos, especially when we understand there were temples and/or altars to Athena, Zeus, Dionysos, Asklepios, the god of healing who was worshiped as a living serpent, as well as to Bacchus, Venus, Apollo, and Minerva.

Commentary

"And to the angel of the church in Pergamos write; These things saith he which hath the sharp sword with two edges" (Rev. 2:12). The word "sword" appears eleven times in the book of Revelation; four times the word has reference to the "sharp two edged sword" of Revelation 1:16. We will have more to say about this "sword" below.

> I know thy works, and where thou dwellest, even where Satan's seat is: and thou holdest fast my name, and hast not denied my faith, even in those days wherein Antipas was my faithful martyr, who was slain among you, where Satan dwelleth (Rev. 2:13).

"I know thy works" is a phrase common in each of the letters to the seven Churches. For those who accept the Bible doctrine of the omniscience of God, this comes as no surprise. He knew their works and if He wrote a letter to the congregation where we attend, He could say the same thing. There is nothing we think, say, or do which can be hid from the all seeing eye of our Lord.

The praise was because they had not denied the faith and were holding fast to the way of righteousness.

Regardless of the trials, tribulations and persecutions they had faced because of the name of Christ, they had remained true to the one faith and were holding fast His name.

The words "where thou dwellest, even where Satan's seat" points to the basic prevailing mindset of the inhabitants of the city. Pergamos held the honor of being the first city in Asia to have the privilege of building a temple dedicated to the worship of the emperors of Rome. As previously stated, they had temples and/or altars to several heathen gods. It was truly a city which would hold afar any religion standing opposed to the idolatry found there.

The word "seat" is from the Greek word thronos, and is translated "throne" fifty-four of the sixty-one times it appears in the New Testament. The word could surely be translated "throne" and do no damage to the message. Hailey said:

> As early as 29 B. C. a temple dedicated to Roma and Augustus was erected in the city as the first and, for a time, the only temple of the imperial cult in all Asia.
> It was followed by a second temple to Trajan and a third to Severus. The city had the distinction of being three times named temple-warden of the state religion,
> before the honor was transferred to Ephesus.3

There is little doubt but that these facts were behind the words of Jesus, "where Satan's seat is."

Furthermore, this deepens our appreciation for the tribute given to the saints, i. e., "thou holdest fast my name, and hast not denied my faith." In spite of a multitude of Satan's stumbling blocks, they had remained true to the call of the cross of Christ. The choice they were forced to make was whether they would say, "Lord Christ" or "Lord Caesar."

Antipas had made his choice. His guidon was "the Lord Jesus Christ." He would not bow to Lord Caesar or any other heathen religion. His eyes were focused on the cross of Christ and he refused to look to the right or to the left.

We know nothing further about Antipas. Some suggest a single individual is not under consideration. The word comes from "anti" (against, to contend against) and "pater" (father). Thus, some propose it could have reference to Christians in Pergamos who stood in opposition to the "emperor worship" existing there.

Regardless of whether the Lord references one man or a group of faithful Christians who refused to deny the faith, their actions were commendable and teach a strong lesson. Those here contemplated (one or many) will hear "Well done, good and faithful servant; thou hast been faithful over a few things, I will make thee ruler over many things: enter thou into the joy of thy lord" (Matt. 25:21, 23). Faithfulness is always in style in God's eyes. There is never a time when Jehovah is not pleased with it.

The Lord knew where they dwelled. He referred to it as "where Satan's seat (throne) is" and "where Satan dwelleth." Pergamos was a place where Satan ruled and reigned, where his will was the banner under which the people of Pergamos, as a whole, walked. The word "dwelleth" here is used in a figurative sense. It refers to the rule, reign, and domination of Satan over the basic mindset of the people in Pergamos.

It sounds as if Jesus was describing America today. Please be assured, I cannot think of anywhere I would rather live than here. But there are many areas of our great country which needs drastic repair. It is not a series of problems curable by the passage of more laws. It is a matter of the heart, of the mind. The religion of Christ is a religion of the will. Righteousness cannot be forced upon one, neither can it be "machine gunned" into a person. It does not come by injection with a hypodermic needle. It flows from the heart of a man who is "poor in spirit" (Matt. 5:3). The words poor in spirit refers to what a man is, not what one has or does not have. It is the man Jeremiah contemplated in the words "O LORD, I know that the way of man is not in himself: it is not in man that walketh to direct his steps" (Jer. 10:23). This poor in spirit man understands that without Divine guidance he is hopeless, helpless, and lost.

Paul wrote "I beseech you therefore, brethren, by the mercies of God, that ye present your bodies a living sacrifice, holy, acceptable unto God, which is your reasonable service" (Rom. 12:1). He calls for service which issues from the reason of man. Woods says, "i.e., a service of the reason, one originating with, and performed by, the reason."4 One chooses to follow the Lord.

> But I have a few things against thee, because thou hast there them that hold the doctrine of Balaam, who taught Balac to cast a stumblingblock before the children of Israel, to eat things sacrificed unto idols, and to commit fornication (Rev. 2:14).

With all the good things Jesus saw in Pergamos, we now discover there were some negative things which needed correction.

Some in the Church at Pergamos had a strong adherence and commitment to the doctrine of Balaam. The details of this doctrine are not known. It is noteworthy that Peter said Balaam "loved the wages of unrighteousness" (2 Pet. 2:15), while Jude referred to "the error of Balaam for reward" (Jude 11). Thus, the root of this doctrine may have been in some way connected to the ever present "love of money" (1 Tim. 6:10).

Possibly Jesus refers to a situation involving a 'stumblingblock." According to Thayer, the word means "Any impediment placed in the way and causing one to stumble or fall, (a stumbling block, occasion of stumbling) i.e. a rock which is a cause of stumbling."5 The charge is that Balaam taught Balak "to cast a stumblingblock before the children of Israel, to eat things sacrificed unto idols, and to commit fornication." The event is revealed in Numbers 25:1-18. Moses references the same thing: "Behold, these caused the children of Israel, through the counsel of Balaam, to commit trespass against the LORD in the matter of Peor, and there was a plague among the congregation of the LORD" (Num. 31:16).

The children of Israel ate things sacrificed to idols. Simply stated, they worshiped idols. They also committed fornication with the women of Moab. Since eating "things sacrificed unto idols" would be spiritual adultery, it seems probable that Jesus here has physical fornication under consideration, especially in light of Numbers 31:15-17.

Regardless of the specifics of Balaam's doctrine in Pergamos, it was "another gospel" (Gal. 1:8-9). There is only one gospel, there is only one faith. There is only one doctrine of Christ. God's people are what they are because of the doctrine of Christ. It is not a creed book, manual, confession of faith, discipline, or catechism that makes us what we are!

It is the doctrine of Christ, nothing more, nothing less and only the doctrine of Christ. "So hast thou also them that hold the doctrine of the Nicolaitans, which thing I hate" (Rev. 2:15).

Some in Pergamos were holding to the "doctrine of the Nicolaitans." The specifics of this doctrine is not known. Some commentators believe those who held the doctrine of the Nicolaitans were the same as those who held the "doctrine of Balaam." Since the Lord said "So hast thou also" (emphasis upon also), leads me to believe there were at least two distinct parties in the Church in Pergamos. Nonetheless, one thing is sure, regardless of whether there was one sect or two, the Lord's displeasure is clearly stated. There can be no doubt but that the saints there knew exactly what the Lord meant.

The severity of the condemnation cannot be missed when we understand the Lord hated this doctrine. The Ephesians were commended because "thou hatest the deeds of the Nicolaitans, which I also hate" (Rev. 2:6). Here, some held "the doctrine of the Nicolaitans, which thing I hate." The "deeds of the Nicolaitans" are different than the "doctrine of the Nicolaitans" only in the thought that doctrine manifests itself in deeds. What one believes is what one does.

Paul commended the Roman Christians because their faith was "spoken of throughout the whole world" (Rom. 1:8). Paul had heard of the Colossian's "faith in Christ Jesus" (Col. 1:4). The saints in Thessalonica were commended because they;

> Were ensamples to all that believe in Macedonia and Achaia. For from you sounded out the word of the Lord not only in Macedonia and Achaia, but also in every place your faith to God-ward is spread abroad; so that we need not to speak any thing (1 Thess. 1:7-8).

These Christians tenaciously held to the once and for all delivered faith (Jude 3). How do we know this? It is simple: Their faith was evidenced in their lives. Conviction manifests itself in deeds. "Repent; or else I will come unto thee quickly, and will fight against them with the sword of my mouth" (Rev. 2:16).

The only alternative was for them to repent. "Repentance" is a change of mind resulting in a changed life. It is "turning from" that which is a violation of God's law and turning to His Divine will. It is cessation of that which is sinful. True repentance is more, much more than mere regret. One can be sorry for his actions, but God demands a change of mind. The changed mind results in a changed life.

The sword here is the rhomphaia. This word is found outside the book of Revelation only once in Luke 2:35. It is said to be of Thracian origin. It was longer and heavier than the machaira, a short sword normally employed by the Romans.

There is no doubt the "sword of my mouth" is the "sword of the Spirit" (Eph. 6:17). The problem our Lord saw would be remedied, but in a way different than the normal uses of a sword. Paul wrote, "For the weapons of our warfare are not carnal, but mighty through God to the pulling down of strong holds;" (2 Cor. 10:4). Man always uses a physical sword whereas the Lord uses the sword which goes forth out of His mouth.

Isaiah saw the difference in the way the new kingdom would spread. When "the mountain of the LORD'S house shall be established in the top of the mountains" (Isa. 2:2), man would see it spread throughout the world in a totally different way than the kingdoms of man spread. In the same reading, Isaiah said,

> And he shall judge among the nations, and shall rebuke many people: and they shall beat their swords into plowshares, and their spears into pruninghooks: nation shall not lift up sword against nation, neither shall they learn war any more (Isa. 2:4).

The nature of the warfare in the Kingdom of Heaven would be much different than the kingdoms of the world. It was one which would not be spread by physical warfare, by clashing armies, the ebb and flow of battle with the clanging of swords, thundering hooves of charging cavalry and the tramping feet of marching infantries.

Jesus said "The kingdom of heaven is like unto leaven, which a woman took, and hid in three measures of meal, till the whole was leavened" (Matt. 13:33). Leaven is silent; it does not move with the accompanying noise of marching troops or the beating of drums. The Hebrew writer affirmed.

> For the word of God is quick, and powerful, and sharper than any twoedged sword, piercing even to the dividing asunder of soul and spirit, and of the joints and marrow, and is a discerner of the thoughts and intents of the heart (Heb. 4:12).

Not all held these doctrines. Why, then, were all told to "repent"? The principle of "A little leaven leaveneth the whole lump" (Gal. 5:9) is here seen. Toleration of evil is a sad thing to behold. Paul told the Corinthian saints," Your glorying is not good. Know ye not that a little leaven leaveneth the whole lump? Purge out therefore the old leaven, that ye may be a new lump...." (1 Cor. 5:6-7). The church at Pergamos was commanded to repent while the Corinthians were told to Purge out the old leaven. When there is sin in the camp, there is always the hope that repentance will be evidenced by the guilty. But when none is seen, the purging out must then come about.

> He that hath an ear, let him hear what the Spirit saith unto the churches; To him that overcometh will I give to eat of the hidden manna, and will give him a white stone, and in the stone a new name written, which no man knoweth saving he that receiveth it (Rev. 2:17)

Let him who has a heart attuned to hearing God's word hear the Spirit's message to the seven Churches of Asia. Let him who WILL hear, hear what the Spirit says to the Churches. The problem here is not the auditory portion of the human anatomy. It is the spiritual senses which are under consideration. Jesus prayed "I thank thee, O Father, Lord of heaven and earth, because thou hast hid these things from the wise and prudent, and hast revealed them unto babes" (Matt. 11:25). The "wise and prudent" are those who the world considers wise and prudent. The "babes" are those who readily receive the word of God.

Jesus told the religious leaders of His day:

> Therefore speak I to them in parables: because they seeing see not; and hearing they hear not, neither do they understand. And in them is fulfilled the prophecy of Esaias, which saith, By hearing ye shall hear, and shall not understand; and seeing ye shall see, and shall not perceive: For this people's heart is waxed gross, and their ears are dull of hearing, and their eyes they have closed; lest at any time they should see with their eyes, and hear with their ears, and should understand with their heart, and should be converted, and I should heal them. But blessed are your eyes, for they see: and your ears, for they hear (Matt. 13:13-16).

God's word is understandable to those who WILL hear it, but is hidden to those who will NOT hear it. There is a direct link between "He that hath an ear" and "the hidden manna." He who hears, and does, is the person who will overcome; the one who overcomes is the one who will receive the hidden manna. The one who hears is the wise man who built his house on a rock (Matt. 7:24).

What is behind the "white stone" is not clear. Many suggestions have been offered through the years, yet none answers every possible problem. Regardless of the various proposals, most commentators agree the state of the Lord's approval is the ultimate picture we are to see. In the book of Revelation, "white" is always associated with the concept on that which is acceptable to God. I see no other possibility here.

Furthermore, Thayer gives additional insight to the "white stone." Relative to the original word rendered stone he writes "In the ancient courts of justice the accused were condemned by black pebbles and the acquitted by white."6 Paul used the word the only other time it is found in the New Testament. In his defense before Agrippa relative to his persecution of the early Church, he said,

> Which thing I also did in Jerusalem: and many of the saints did I shut up in prison, having received authority from the chief priests; and when they were put to death, I gave my voice against them (Acts 26:10).

The word "voice" is the focus of our attention. Thus, Paul "voiced" (voted; figuratively, he cast in a black stone) his judgment the person on trial was worthy of death.

A great amount has been written concerning the "new name." The focal point of most has been the custom or tradition the Lord might have been drawing upon in this illustration. We know that "name" is sometimes used to describe all that pertains to the individual. Since the context is one of "overcoming," it possibly has reference to the faithful person and their relationship to their Lord, standing approved, accepted and cherished.

Regardless of the background of this illustration, we are keenly aware the person referenced in verse seventeen is the one who has victoriously faced the trials and tribulations ushered in because of the name they wore. Just as they would meet the Lord's approval, so will those who, in the 21st Century, victoriously meet and overcome.

STUDY QUESTIONS

1. In the city of Pergamos, there were altars to Athena, Zeus, Dionysos, Asklepios, Bacchus, Venus, Apollo, and Minerva. What are some of the things John wrote to the Church in Pergamos which draws our attention to this fact?
2. Discuss the importance of John's statement "where Satan's seat is."
3. How important is John's statement "where Satan dwelleth" in light of all that he said, both positively and negatively, about the Church in Pergamos?
4. How are we to understand that Satan 'dwelled' in Pergamos?
5. Unto which of the churches did John affirm that Jesus knew their works?
6. When considering the many heathen gods to which the people in Pergamos had raised an idol, can we see any similarities to America today?
7. Discuss the phrase "which is your reasonable service" in Romans 12:1.
8. Discuss the significance of Jesus' hatred for the "doctrine of the Nicolaitans."
9. In this lesson I wrote, "The 'deeds of the Nicolaitans' are different than the 'doctrine of the Nicolaitans' only in the thought that doctrine manifests itself in deeds. What one believes is what one does." Do you agree with that statement? If so, why? If not, why?
10. Discuss the concept of "repentance" as it related to the Christians in Pergamos and as it relates to us today.

WORKS CITED

The Latter Rain Page—http://latter-rain.com/escha/pergam.htm
Ibid.

Homer Hailey, Revelation An Introduction and Commentary (Grand Rapids: Baker Book House, 1983) p. 129.

Guy N. Woods, A Commentary on the New Testament Epistles of Peter, John, and Jude (Nashville, TN: Gospel Advocate Company, 1964), p. 55.

Joseph Henry Thayer, Greek-English Lexicon of the New Testament, Electronic Database (BibleWorks, 2007).
Thayer, ibid.

The Church at Philadelphia

The Churches OF THE New Testament

INTRODUCTION

The Philadelphia congregation is mentioned in only two New Testament chapters—Revelation 1 and 3. It is named in chapter one; the epistle directed to this Asiatic congregation is given in Revelation 3:7-13. It (Philadelphia) and the one (church) at Smyrna stand on the mountain peaks of spiritual excellence; four are below these two; the other, Laodicea, is far below its neighbor to the northwest—Philadelphia. Four of these congregations receive commendation and censure. Two, Smyrna and Philadelphia, receive only commendation. One, Laodicea, received only censure. These five could have climbed to the spiritual stature of the two faithful ones; they chose not to do so which is sad, inexpressibly so. Laodicea chose lukewarmness over fervency.

THE CITY OF PHILADELPHIA

This city was located about 25 to 30 miles southeast of Sardis; 85 miles east of Smyrna, and 75 miles northwest of Laodicea. However, the spiritual distance between lukewarm Laodicea and faithful, fervent Philadelphia was astronomical. They were not on the same spiritual wave length at all.

It (Philadelphia) was a newer city than the other six. It was built in second century B. C. by Attalus II. He named it Philadelphia in devoted honor to his brother—Eumenes—whom he greatly loved and deeply admired. The name has a noble connotation, meaning brotherly love. Hence, it was the city of brotherly love. Jews who made up the synagogue in Philadelphia, did not live up to that noble name at all. They acted as if it were the city of brotherly hatred.

They were physical descendants of Abraham, having his blood coursing their veins. They were not kin to him spiritually at all! In marked contrast, Christians were his spiritual descendants having Christ's blood coursing their veins. The former had no time for the latter.

Philadelphia was home to many temples and public buildings. It earned the title of "Little Athens." An excellent climate prevailed and the fertility of the soil made it conducive to grape growing. One, therefore, is not surprised to learn the god of wine, Bacchus (Greek) or Dionysus (Roman) was of chief importance there.

This city was located near where Lydia, Mysia and Phrygia converged. Situated on an important highway running west and east made it a marketing success. Many people passed through this city on a daily basis. The city had a Greek mission to accomplish. It had been established to spread the Greek way of life inclusive of the Grecian language and the Greek culture. It desired to "Grecianize" that whole area. Christ had other plans for that city. He desired the church to be a radiating center for the outreach of truth. This was the stimulating challenge He held before the church in Revelation 3:8—an open door for the gospel's spread.

A THREEFOLD DESCRIPTION OF JESUS CHRIST

As true with the previous five letters, Jesus gives an assessment of Himself. Verse 7 reads,
> And to the angel of the church in Philadelphia write, These things saith he that is holy, he that is true, he that hath the key of David, he that openeth, and no more shutteth; and shutteth, and no man openeth;...

(1) He is the holy One. Israel, in the Old Testament, was told with frequency, they were to be holy (Exod. 19:6; Lev. 11:44-45). Spiritual Israel is told the same in 1 Peter 1:16. Hebrews 7:26 affirms Him to be "holy, harmless, undefiled, separate from sinners, and made higher than the heavens." The apostles in Acts 4:27 referred to Him as the "holy child Jesus,..." No sin or impurity ever sullied or soiled His immaculate character.

Pilate and his wife found no fault in Him (Luke 23:14; Matt. 27:19). Neither did Paul, Peter nor John detect any fault or flaw in Him (2 Cor. 5:21; 1 Pet. 2:22; 1 John 3:5).

(2) He is true. He is truth personified. He is "the way, the truth and the life" (John 14:6). This is one of the great "I am" declarations of John's gospel record. Pilate asked in John 18:37, "What is truth?" Living truth or embodied truth in all excellent essence stood before him and he (did not) realized it not. He did not wait for an answer!

(3) He possesses the key of David. This is an evident allusion to Isaiah 22:22. Keys symbolize authority and He possesses it both in heaven and on earth as per Matthew 28:18. Keys permit entrance; they forbid entrance of the unworthy. Jesus opens; no man can close. He closes; no man can open. His enemies are totally powerless in assailing successfully the authoritative sway of His reign. This meant He was/is the true Messiah. He occupied David's throne then; He still does today. The Jewish synagogue of Satan was unhappy. It brings no solace to premillennialists who deny Him a current throne. They want a future, not a present one. Down, DOWN goes this materialistic madness that has captured multiplied millions into its visionary grasp and grip. Premillennialism has a totally different Jesus than Philadelphia had and we have currently.

JESUS KNEW THEIR WORKS

Verse 8 states,
I know thy works: behold, I have set before thee an open door, and no man can shut it: for thou has a little strength, and hast kept my word, and hast not denied my name.

Unlike the condemned works in Sardis, already mentioned and Laodicea subsequently to be portrayed with pity, Jesus recognized their commended works. No censure of them is given. They line up with stalwart Smyrna of Revelation 2 in the fully dedicated department.

He who possessed the key of David had placed before them an opened door. This, very likely, was an opened door for evangelistic expansion.

The Church At Philadelphia

Be it recalled that the new city of Philadelphia had been established to be an opened door for the expansion of Hellenism (Greek culture) into the provinces of Lydia, Mysia and Phyrgia. Theirs was a spiritual door opened. The open door occurs a number of times in the New Testament. A door of faith had been opened for Paul and Barnabas on missionary journey number one (Acts 14:27). A great door and effectual was opened for Paul at Ephesus (1 Cor. 16:8-9). There was an opened (open) door for Paul at Troas in 2 Corinthians 2:12. Paul desired "a door of utterance" be opened for him in Colossians 4:2. Granted to stalwart saints in the city of brotherly love was an opened door for the expansion of Christian culture—not Grecian culture. Their enemies would be impotent in its closure.

They had a little strength. This meant they were small and struggling. His word had been stedfastly sustained. This was the positive and plus side of militant Christianity in the face of their foes.

They had not denied His name. This was their noble negative of extended commendation. The name stood for the all of Christ. Their unbending support of Him had been thorough. It had not lagged. How wonderful when such can be said. Here is a positive and a negative in perfect balance.

Verse 9 states,

> Behold, I will make them of the synagogue of Satan, which say they are Jews, and are not, but do lie; behold, I will make them to come and worship before thy feet, and to know that I have loved thee.

Satan stays on 24/7 alert toward God's people who take a strong stand in behalf of saving truth. This was true among churches in Asia who were waging relentlessly and resolutely a war of righteousness and godliness. Satan had his synagogue at Smyrna and Philadelphia. He had his seat at Pergamos. The depths of Satanic sinfulness were faced by those in Thyatira who had not known his wily ways, his skilled strategies (Rev. 2:24-25).

Jesus came to spiritual grips promptly and powerfully in labeling one of the grievous wrongs afflicting struggling saints in Philadelphia—infidelic, militant Jews who hated Christ, His gospel and His people.

In this assessment Jesus is totally unlike Protestant premillennial proponents of our day who run with the ball for unbelieving Jews currently and call them the special people of God. Yet, these same infidelic Jews of our era hate Jesus Christ, label Him an imposter, declare that the New Testament ought not be in the Bible at all and deny the church of Christ of its eternal nature and its divine derivation. Yet, we are assured by these diehard millennialists that such people belong to God by special ownership, in a way no others do or can do. How pathetic to be of such persuasion.

This was not the Lord's assessment of such infidelic Jews at Philadelphia. He placed such people in Satan's corner—not His or the Father's corner. They formed Satan's synagogue—not the Saviour's church. They professed to be Jews but Christ denied their invalid claims. They were totally unworthy of being even Abrahamic descendants physically, to say nothing of being Abrahamic descendants spiritually. They lost out on both scores. Jesus called them liars, people void of truth. Liars, whether Jews or Gentiles, are not approved children of God and disciples of the Christ. Such people, as they were, are hell-bound as per Revelation 21:8 and 22:15. Truth did not verify their counterfeit claims.

Jesus promised God's real people at Philadelphia—Christians—He would see to it that such misguided zealots would come and worship before their feet and to know of His love for afflicted saints of the Most High God and His only begotten Son. Though this may refer to what these Jewish enemies would do and acknowledge if they ever became Christians, yet it seems much more likely that this synagogue of Satan filled with professing Jews, ultimately will come to see and sense who God's people actually are, and yet still refuse to hear and heed the truth as it is situated in Jesus Christ. In the strongest of measures, Jesus assured His persecuted people that infidelity will end and He and His Cause will experience an eternal victory. This, in essence, is the meaning of eternal life promised the sure and stedfast in Smyrna.

Have militant millennialists never read and contemplated Revelation 3:9? They need to park at this passage and remain there until beautiful belief replaces their blind prejudice toward faithless Jews who are not God's people today.

PROMISES VOUCHSAFED THEM

Verse 10 states,
> Because thou hast kept the word of my patience, I also will keep thee from the hour of temptation, which shall come upon all the world, to try them that dwell upon the earth.

Philadelphia saints had kept the word of Jesus' patience. They were doing what Jesus counseled in Luke 21:19, "In your patience possess ye your souls." The Royal Redeemer now reciprocates with a precious promise. In powerful fashion He will keep them intact with His own brand of protection when the hour of temptation faces them and comes upon the whole world for testing purposes. Quite obviously, the hour refers to a session of strict trying and sure testing. Christians have never been free from the onslaughts of persecution (Matt. 5:10-12; 2 Tim. 3:12). Trials have always beset God's people. Every generation of stalwarts so attests. Those who endure successfully will receive a crown of life of which James and John wrote respectively (Jam. 1:12; 2 John 8; Rev. 2:10).

John wrote in verse 11, "Behold, I come quickly: hold that fast, that no man take thy crown. His coming quickly is no allusion to the second coming for that event was far off in A. D. 96 and may well be in the far distant future from our vantage point of time in 2010. There are no signs of a near coming that some claim now to see. He would come quickly to aid them and protect them as promised in verse 10. It was not all in Deity's corner. They had a part to play. They were to hold fast or cling tenaciously to what they had. At all costs they were to make doubly sure that no man take their crown and cause them to forfeit the heavenly inheritance of which they, if faithful, would be the rich heirs.

More of His precious promises occur in verse 12 wherein we read,
> Him that overcometh will I make a pillar in the temple of my God, and he shall go no more out: and I will write upon him the name of my God, and the name of the city of my God, which is new Jerusalem, which cometh down out of heaven from my God: and I will write upon him my new name.

Each of the seven letters contains an earnest encouragement to overcome. Johnny Ramsey was fond of saying, "If you will overcome, you may come over and live with Me." The overcomer will be made a pillar in God's temple. Though some think this is a reference to the temple or church in the here and now, it is far more plausible to view it as a reference to the Heavenly temple. Portrayed here is permanence. Philadelphia had a history of experiencing earthquakes which called for an evacuation of the city and an accompanying dread of returning. Blessed assurance is offered that such will never occur in heaven. There will be permanence and eternal security.

The redeemed saint in heaven will be the recipient of a threefold name stamped upon him/her. Jesus will do the inscribing. (1) He will inscribe the Father's name. What a great honor this will be! (2) The name of the Heavenly City will be inscribed. This is the new Jerusalem. The old Jerusalem had been destroyed 26 years earlier or in A. D. 70. It will be called the same in Revelation 21:2. This suggests citizenship. (3) Jesus will write upon the heavenly heir His own new name. It, plus the Father's name, adds up to divine ownership. These august names add up to all these Divine Persons are. What marvelous motivation is provided for the courageous overcomer.

Verse 13 reads, "He that hath an ear, let him hear what the Spirit saith unto the churches." This divine demand is part and parcel of all these seven letters. Jesus provides the essence of what we are to hear. We are to activate it into attitude and action, into language and life, into motive and mission.

SEVEN LESSONS LEARNED

1. In the Captain of our salvation we have the very personification of holiness and truth.
2. He who has the key of David now occupies David's throne which refutes resoundingly lethal premillennialism.
3. God's people should be interested in every door of opportunity to advance His Cause.

4. Lying Jews who hate Jesus and despise Christianity are not God's special people by any stretch of the imagination.

5. All enemies of Jesus sooner or later will acknowledge both Him and His people.

6. Jesus is the keeper of those who keep His Word.

7. Heaven is a place of permanence and security for the redeemed.

STUDY QUESTIONS

1. What is unique about Smyrna and Philadelphia in Revelation 2 and 3?
2. Give the background of the city.
3. Discuss the threefold portrait given by Jesus of Himself.
4. Discuss open door passages in Acts 14; 1 Corinthians 16; 2 Corinthians 2; Colossians 4 and in Revelation 3.
5. In what ways had they exhibited their faithfulness and ardency?
6. How are Jews assessed by Jesus in Revelation 3:9?
7. What could diehard pre-millennialists learn, if they were willing, from Revelation 3:9?
8. What promise of provision and protection is vouchsafed them in Revelation 3:10?
9. Read and discuss Revelation 3:11.
10. What rewards are promised overcomers in Revelation 3:12?

Endnotes

All quotations are from the KJV unless otherwise noted.

Robert R. Taylor, Jr., Philadelphia: The Church With An Open Door, Annual Denton Lectures, Studies In The Revelation, Dub McClish, Editor (Delight, Arkansas, Valid Publications, Inc., 1984) pp. 112-116

The Churches of the New Testament
The Church at Philippi

INTRODUCTION

The New Testament contains a tremendous amount of information written about, as well as to, various congregations in the first century. To illustrate, Luke wrote at length in Acts about the Jerusalem congregation. Also, letters [epistles] were addressed to the congregations in Rome, Corinth, Galatia, Ephesus, etc. By carefully studying and rightly dividing this information relating to churches in the first century, we can know the Lord's will for His church today.

The congregation in Philippi is unlike some of the other New Testament churches. Luke wrote about its establishment in Acts, and the apostle Paul wrote a letter to its members [Philippians]. The main sections of this lesson are based on these two sources of information.

LUKE WROTE ABOUT THE ESTABLISHMENT OF THE CHURCH IN PHILIPPI IN ACTS

The church in Philippi was established as the Great Commission was being fulfilled. Just before He ascended to heaven, Jesus instructed His apostles to "teach all nations" (Matt. 28:19-20). According to Mark's account, they were to "preach the gospel to every creature" (Mk. 16:15-16). This may seem like an overwhelming task for a few men to accomplish. However, Jesus actually gave the apostles a step by step plan: "ye shall be witnesses unto me both in Jerusalem, and in all Judea, and in Samaria, and unto the uttermost part of the earth" (Acts 1:8).

The Church At Phillipi

The apostles began their work in Jerusalem, and a great and growing congregation was established in that city (Acts 2-6). Eventually, persecution caused many Christians to scatter "throughout the regions of Judea and Samaria" (Acts 8:1). As these brethren left Jerusalem, they "went every where preaching the word" (Acts 8:4). Please note how the Great Commission was being fulfilled, and how other disciples, besides the apostles, became involved.

An especially significant conversion is recorded in Acts 9. Saul, a persecutor of the church, became a Christian. Saul's conversion is significant because the Lord selected him to accomplish a special work among Gentiles (Acts 9:15; 22:21; 26:17). Some time later Barnabas brought Saul to Antioch where they served the Lord together (Acts 11:25-26). We learn from Acts 13:1-3 the church in Antioch sent Barnabas and Saul [Paul] on a missionary journey to do the work they had been called to do.

Paul began his second missionary journey with Silas when he parted company with Barnabas in Antioch (Acts 15:36-41). After being joined by Timothy, Paul was forbidden by the Spirit to go to certain areas (Acts 16:1-7). In Troas Paul received his Macedonian call, and he traveled to Philippi, having been joined by Luke (Acts 16:8-12). Thus, the Lord sent Paul, accompanied by Silas, Timothy, and Luke to Europe. The Great Commission continued to be carried out as Paul and his co-workers made their way to Philippi. We read about the establishment of the Philippian congregation in Acts 16:13-40.

Soon after entering a city, Paul customarily went to the synagogue. It seems Philippi had no synagogue, so he went to a river where people gathered for prayer, and he talked with some women (v. 13). This meeting led to the conversion of Lydia and her household (vs. 14-15). Following this positive beginning, Paul and Silas were abused and put in prison because Paul cast a spirit out of a young woman (vs. 16-24). They reacted by praying and singing praises to God (v. 25). A great earthquake led to an opportunity to teach the jailer, and he and his household were converted (vs. 26-34). When Lydia, the jailer, and their households were saved, the Lord added them to His church (Acts 2:47). Together they formed a congregation in which they worshipped and served the Lord.

After considering Luke's record of the Philippian church's establishment, let us be reminded the Great Commission is still in effect. God's people are responsible for sending preachers to spread the Gospel so others can learn it, believe it, obey it, and be saved. In Romans 10:11-17 we read:

> For the scripture saith, Whosoever believeth on him shall not be ashamed. For there is no difference between the Jew and the Greek: for the same Lord over all is rich unto all that call upon him. For whosoever shall call upon the name of the Lord shall be saved. How then shall they call on him in whom they have not believed? and how shall they believe in him of whom they have not heard? and how shall they hear without a preacher? And how shall they preach, except they be sent? as it is written, How beautiful are the feet of them that preach the gospel of peace, and bring glad tidings of good things! But they have not all obeyed the gospel. For Esaias saith, Lord, who hath believed our report? So then faith cometh by hearing, and hearing by the word of God.

Perhaps we also need to be reminded God will lead His followers in carrying out the Great Commission. In no way are we implying the Spirit communicates directly with Christians today or that the Lord reveals His will through visions as He did with Paul. However, Solomon showed long ago how God leads providentially when he wrote: "Trust in the Lord with all thine heart; and lean not unto thine own understanding. In all thy ways acknowledge him, and he shall direct thy paths" (Prov. 3:5-6). In connection with the Lord's providential leading, let us keep in mind He is the giver and the taker of opportunity (Rev. 3:7-8).

Although Paul and Silas were treated unlawfully as Roman citizens in Philippi, they left that city to carry on their work in other areas (Acts 16:35-40). Paul stayed in contact with the Christians in Philippi, and they developed an extremely strong, loving relationship. This brings us to the second main section of this lecture.

PAUL WROTE A LETTER TO THE CHURCH IN PHILIPPI

Paul's letter reveals a number of characteristics the Lord wants His church to possess. These characteristics can be learned from the example set by the church in Philippi as well as from the instructions given to its members. Although this is by no means an exhaustive list, we are concentrating on six such traits, including three from the Philippian church's example and three from Paul's instructions.

THE EXAMPLE OF THE CHURCH IN PHILIPPI

First, the church in Philippi shows how the Lord wants each congregation to be organized. Paul addressed his letter "to all the saints in Christ Jesus which are at Philippi, with the bishops and deacons" (Phil. 1:1). We observed earlier that the church is composed of "the saved" [saints in Christ] who have been added to it by the Lord (Acts 2:47). Please note the Philippian church's membership included "bishops" and "deacons."

The Scriptures clearly teach each congregation is to be led by a special group of men (Acts 14:23; Tit. 1:5). The men who serve as bishops are also called "elders" (Acts 14:23), "overseers" (Acts 20:28), and "pastors" (Eph. 4:11). To serve in this capacity, men must meet certain qualifications (1 Tim. 3:1-7; Tit. 1:5-9). The gravity of these qualifications will be more fully appreciated when we properly understand the weighty responsibilities assigned to congregational leaders (Acts 20:28; Tit. 1:9-11; Heb. 13:17; Jas. 5:14; 1 Pet. 5:1-3).

In addition to being led by bishops, each congregation is to be served by a special group of men called "deacons." To be appointed as deacons, men must meet the qualifications listed in 1 Timothy 3:8-13. Practical insight concerning the appointment and work of deacons can be gained from the selection of seven men to serve the Jerusalem church (Acts 6:1-7).

The church in Philippi deserves recognition for developing bishops and deacons in a relatively brief period of time. We believe Paul first went to Philippi around 52 AD, and he wrote Philippians in 63 AD. Thus, the congregation in Philippi was scripturally organized within about 10-12 years after it was established.

Second, the church in Philippi shows how the Lord wants each congregation to be known for its "love." As he introduced his letter Paul wrote: "And this I pray, that your love may abound yet more and more in knowledge and in all judgment" (Phil. 1:9). Why is love such an important trait for the Lord's church? Jesus answered this question when He said:
> A new commandment I give unto you, That ye love one another; as I have loved you, that ye also love one another. By this shall all men know that ye are my disciples, if ye have love one to another (John 13:34-35).

Third, the church in Philippi shows how the Lord wants each congregation to support those who preach the Gospel. Paul highly commended the brethren in Philippi for their generous financial assistance. In the conclusion to his letter he wrote:
> Now ye Philippians know also, that in the beginning of the gospel, when I departed from Macedonia, no church communicated with me as concerning giving and receiving, but ye only. For even in Thessalonica ye sent once and again unto my necessity (Phil. 4:15-16).

Through their financial support the Christians in Philippi had "fellowship in the gospel" (Phil. 1:5) with Paul. Maybe this will help us to better appreciate why he said, "I thank my God upon every remembrance of you" (Phil. 1:3).

For three additional characteristics the Lord wants His church to possess, let us turn our attention to.

PAUL'S INSTRUCTIONS TO THE CHURCH IN PHILIPPI

Fourth, Paul's instructions in Philippians indicate the Lord wants His church to be united. Note the following plea:
> Only let your conversation be as it becometh the gospel of Christ: that whether I come and see you, or else be absent, I may hear of your affairs, that ye stand fast in one spirit, with one mind striving together for the faith of the gospel (Phil. 1:27).

Why is unity so important? David and Jesus answered this question. According to David, brethren dwelling together in unity is both good and pleasant (Psa. 133:1). Also, in the shadow of the cross, Jesus prayed His followers would be one, as He and the Father are one (John 17:11, 20-23).

Regretfully, even though the church in Philippi was an ideal congregation composed of saints who were commended for their love, two members were at odds with each other. This situation led Paul to write: "I beseech Euodias, and beseech Syntyche, that they be of the same mind in the Lord" (Phil. 4:2). Imagine the shame of being called out by name in Paul's letter of joy. We do not know the cause of their contention, but we do know harmony could have existed between Euodias and Syntyche if they would have practiced the following instructions:

> If there be therefore any consolation in Christ, if any comfort of love, if any fellowship of the Spirit, if any bowels and mercies, fulfill ye my joy, that ye be likeminded, having the same love, being of one accord, of one mind. Let nothing be done through strife or vainglory; but in lowliness of mind let each esteem other better than themselves. Look not every man on his own things, but every man also on the things of others (Phil. 2:1-4).

We can only hope that Euodias and Syntyche reconciled like Jacob and Esau (Gen. 33:1-4). The Lord certainly is pleased when His people are united, but He has special contempt for one who sows discord among brethren (Prov. 6:16-19).

Fifth, Paul's instructions in Philippians indicate the Lord wants His church to beware of false teachers. Note this warning: "Beware of dogs, beware of evil workers, beware of the concision" (Phil. 3:2). The conversion of Gentiles to Christ in cities such as Philippi produced great joy. Unfortunately, certain Jewish teachers harassed Gentile Christians, insisting they be circumcised and keep the Law of Moses. This issue was settled in Jerusalem (Acts 15:1-32), but the continued efforts of these teachers caused Paul to issue this strong warning. He continued by stating:

> For many walk, of whom I have told you often, and now tell you even weeping, that they are the enemies of the cross of Christ: whose end is destruction, whose God is their belly, and whose glory is in their shame, who mind earthly things (Phil. 3:18-19).

God's people face different issues today, but we must heed the same warning because false teachers still abound. Several years ago a brother appealed to the following verses from Paul's letter in an attempt to justify teaching incorrect doctrine:

> Some indeed preach Christ even of envy and strife; and some also of good will: the one preach Christ of contention, not sincerely, supposing to add affliction to my bonds: but the other of love, knowing that I am set for the defence of the gospel. What then? notwithstanding, every way, whether in pretence, or in truth, Christ is preached; and I therein do rejoice, yea, and will rejoice (Phil. 1:15-18).

His interpretation was that Paul was not upset when brethren did not preach the same message he preached. Fortunately, I had heard this ridiculous argument before and was able to answer it. Why would Paul justify teaching incorrect doctrine and later in the same letter warn against it? The message under consideration in these verses is "Christ," not false doctrine. Paul was showing how people preached Christ from a variety of motives. Paul did not rejoice when teachers presented false messages, and neither should we.

Sixth, Paul's instructions in Philippians indicate the Lord wants joy to abound in His church. "Finally, my brethren, rejoice in the Lord" (Phil. 3:1). "Rejoice in the Lord alway: and again I say, Rejoice" (Phil. 4:4). The joy under consideration is not an outward expression of happiness based on pleasant circumstances. This kind of joy cannot be experienced "always." The joy Paul dealt with is an inner peace of mind that is based on having a right relationship with the Lord. This kind of joy can be experienced "always," in spite of unpleasant circumstances. To illustrate, Paul and Silas demonstrated true joy when they prayed and sang praises to God after being beaten and locked up in prison (Acts 16:25).

We are fortunate to have additional instructions that will enable us to always rejoice in the Lord. Let us examine them (Phil. 4:5-9).

"Let your 'moderation' [forbearance] be known unto all men" (v. 5). Moderation is a key ingredient of joy.

Someone who is quick tempered and outspoken does not radiate joy. Christians allow their moderation to be known by practicing forbearance when dealing with others. As motivation to practice forbearance, we are reminded the Lord is "at hand." Christ is near to help His people, and He has provided the proper example to imitate.

"Be 'careful' [anxious] for nothing; but in every thing by prayer and supplication with thanksgiving let your requests be made known unto God" (v. 6). Anxiety destroys joy. Thankfully, the Lord has given us an alternative. Rather than be filled with anxiety, we are to make our requests known to God through prayer. However, as we ask God to supply our needs we are to do so with gratitude.

> Finally, brethren, whatsoever things are true, whatsoever things are honest, whatsoever things are just, whatsoever things are pure, whatsoever things are lovely, whatsoever things are of good report; if there be any virtue, and if there be any praise, think on these things (v. 8).

Our thought patterns determine what we say, what we do, and the way we act: "For as he thinketh in his heart, so is he" (Prov. 23:7). In order to have hearts filled with joy, we must think properly. Eight beautiful categories of things to think on are listed.

Those who practice these instructions will enjoy two special blessings. "And the peace of God, which passeth all understanding, shall keep your hearts and minds through Christ Jesus" (v. 7). "Those things, which ye have both learned, and received, and heard, and seen in me, do: and the God of peace shall be with you" (v. 9). Can there possibly be a better description of "joy" than having the peace of God keep our hearts and minds and having the God of peace to be with us? People in the world need to see true joy in the church. In this regard, let us heed the following admonition:

> Do all things without murmurings and disputings: that ye may be blameless and harmless, the sons of God, without rebuke, in the midst of a crooked and perverse nation, among whom ye shine as lights in the world (Phil. 2:14-15).

CONCLUSION

The establishment of the congregation in Philippi shows how churches of Christ [not different religious groups or denominations] are produced when Christians faithfully carry out the Great Commission. The example of the Philippian congregation shows how the Lord wants His church to be organized, to be known for its love, and to support those who preach. Paul's instructions in Philippians show how the Lord wants His church to be united, to beware of false teachers, and to always rejoice in Him.

May the following message encourage us to implement these principles as we continue in the great work of restoring the New Testament church!

> For our conversation is in heaven: from whence also we look for the Saviour, the Lord Jesus Christ: who shall change our vile body, that it may be fashioned like unto his glorious body, according to the working whereby he is able even to subdue all things unto himself (Phil. 3:20-21).

STUDY QUESTIONS

1. Paul had a vision in Troas. What did the man in the vision request of him?
2. When Paul arrived in Philippi, where were people assembling for prayer?
3. Who were the first converts to Christianity in Philippi?
4. Why were Paul and Silas put in prison in Philippi?
5. What did Paul and Silas do in prison at midnight?
6. How was the congregation in Philippi organized?
7. What was Paul's admonition for Euodias and Syntyche?
8. What are the keys to rejoicing in the Lord always?
9. What is the alternative to anxiety?
10. On what kinds of things are Christians to think?

The Church at Colosse

The Churches OF THE New Testament

INTRODUCTION

Ephesians and Colossians are twin epistles penned by Paul while in Rome the first time. The theme of Ephesians is "The church of Christ." The theme of Colossians is, "The Christ of the church." In both he spoke concerning Christ and the church as per Ephesians 5:32. Our assigned topic is "The church in Colosse."

THE CITY OF COLOSSE

Colosse is the spelling in the KJV; Colossae is the spelling in the ASV of 1901. The KJV spelling will be observed in this chapter.

Colosse was an Asiatic city located about 100 miles east of Ephesus. Neighboring cities were Laodicea and Hierapolis. All three of these were some six to twelve miles of each other. Laodicea is mentioned only in the Colossian epistle and the book of Revelation. Paul, in Colossians, does not portray it as lukewarm as John surely did in Revelation 3:14-22. Hierapolis is mentioned in no other book than Colossians. These three cities were located in the Lycus Valley area of Asia Minor—now modern day Turkey.

Colosse, in earlier times, had been a greater and more prominent city than it was in the A. D. 60's. It was home to Phrygian people, Greeks and Jews. It was more pagan than pious. It was far more sensual than spiritual. It was situated among idolatrous surroundings and among worshippers of idols.

Among idols worshipped were Bacchus and Cybele. Bacchus was the god of wine while Cybele supposedly was the mother of the gods. Both idols were worshipped with the most shameful of sexual orgies. Men and women consorted freely and frequently without any shame attached. Lusts of flesh and eyes triggered such in attitude and action.

Pride, the other ingredient of worldliness as per 1 John 2:15-17, played its role as men boasted of their sexual conquests and women took pride in the number of sexual partners they had experienced. It was debauchery gone to seed!

Christianity, the gospel of moral purity and soul redemption, had an uphill battle in this cesspool of corruption, this city of intense indulgence.

THE ESTABLISHMENT OF THE COLOSSIAN CONGREGATION

It is highly unlikely Paul established this congregation directly as he did so many others on his historic missionary journeys. In Colossians 2:1 he seemingly exempts himself from firsthand knowledge of the Colossians in a face-to-face way.

During the eventful years he spent in Ephesus, Acts 19, there was a wide sweep of gospel evangelization. Luke attests to this in Acts 19:10. It may have been in this time frame that Epaphras and Philemon were converted. They both were connected with the Colossian congregation as a thorough contemplation of Colossians and Philemon will indicate. One of these, or perhaps both, may have been instrumental in the establishment of the congregation at Colosse. Regardless of its founder or founders, we are grateful for its beginning and the faith, love and hope exemplified there as delightfully depicted in the marvelous missive to them.

THE WRITER OF COLOSSIANS

Paul is the opening word both in our English version and in the original Greek. Minus doubt or debate to the contrary, he was the earthly penman with the Holy Spirit as the heavenly author. There is an apostolic flavor permeating the four chapters and the ninety-five verses of this inspired composition.

The church of Colosse was composed partly, if not largely, of Gentiles or Greeks. Paul was the apostle of the Gentiles as stated clearly by him in Romans 11:13. Earlier, he had stated that "the care of all the churches" rested on his Herculean shoulders (2 Cor. 11:28). This, surely, would be inclusive of the Colossian congregation.

THE DATE, CIRCUMSTANCES AND LOCATION OF ITS COMPOSITION

Paul was imprisoned in Rome from A. D. 61-63. Perhaps A. D. 52 would be the writing date. Perhaps it, and Ephesians, a twin epistle, were written about the same time.

Paul was a prisoner in Rome at the time he penned this mighty missive. Chained to a Praetorian guard (Philippians 1:13-ASV) did not chill his ardor or curtail his outreach with God's glorious gospel. His pen was potent. He still touches lives in powerful ways through his writings. Acts 28:16,23,30 shed light about his lodging arrangements and the duration of his first Roman imprisonment.

THE "WHY" OF ITS COMPOSITION

Serious problems faced Colossian saints. Seemingly, this is why Epaphras made the long, perilous trip to Rome to seek personally Paul's sage counsel. Trouble was brewing from Docetic and Cerinthian Gnostics. The former denied Jesus came in the flesh; the latter differentiated between Jesus and Christ saying Christ came on Jesus at His baptism and vacated Him at His crucifixion. Fatal errors from paganism, asceticism, Gnosticism and Judaism converged on this congregation. Some of the false teachers there contended there were aeons between Christ and God. Furthermore, it was their contention that Christ was not all they needed. In slanderous terms they said He was incomplete and insufficient in the redeeming realm, the saving sphere.

They needed much instruction relative to Christ, the church, morality and daily living for God, Christ and the Holy Spirit. Paul wanted them to be "in the know" about what was transpiring for him in Rome as a prisoner of the Lord Jesus. Tychicus and Onesimus would be the informants relative to this momentous matter.

Paul's magnanimous heart reached not to them alone but to neighboring Laodicea and Hierapolis as well. He loved "the brotherhood" as Peter penned in 1 Peter 2:17. He did not say love your home congregation and no one else. Too many among us have adopted this very narrow concept.

Paul commended his fellow laborers in high tones permeated with the deepest of appreciation. Paul loved and respected them and wanted a reciprocation of such from Colossian Christians. Unrequited love, such as Paul experienced from Corinth in 2 Corinthians 12:15, was not to his apostolic approval at all!

HIGHLIGHTS FROM COLOSSIANS 1

In verses 1-2 we have the Pauline salutation. Paul is an apostle. Timothy's name is affixed though he was not a co-writer of this letter. He is Paul's brother and also theirs. The addressees are "saints and faithful brethren" at Colosse. Grace and peace are bequeathed them coming from the Father and Son. Paul was no oneness Holiness preacher or writer. He knew there were three in the Godhead—not just one—not just Jesus only.

In verse 3 we have a marvelous manifestation of gratitude expressed and prayers rendered in their behalf.

In verses 4-5 we have Paul's famous and favored triad—faith, love, and hope in that order. See 1 Thessalonians 5:8 and 1 Corinthians 13:13 for other apostolic allusions to these famed traits of Christian character.

Fruit-bearing comes in for apostolic emphasis in verse 6. They became fruit-bearers from conversion onward. Paul links truth and grace. Men today separate them with much talk about grace while ignoring the royal ramifications of kingly truth.

In verses 7-8 Epaphras is commended most highly. He has aided Paul in knowing the Colossian mindset and their daily decorum.

In verses 9-12 we have a rich insight into Paul's prayerful concern for them. The content of Paul's prayers for them is refreshing—one we should imitate on a daily basis. Gratitude emerges again in verse 12.

In verses 13-14 we have their conversion portrayed in apostolic colors. They had been delivered. They had been translated into the kingdom. Their redemption is royally riveted to Christ's crimson blood—His precious blood, His powerful blood.

The goodness, greatness and grandeur of Christ shines brightly and brilliantly in verse 15-19. These verses refuted errors taught the Colossians. They answered the blatant attacks made against Christ from those who bashed Him relentlessly.

Reconciliation comes into powerful play in verses 20-22. Verse 23 presents the wide sweep of the gospel in Paul's day. It had gone world-wide much like Paul wrote in Romans 10:18.

In verses 24-26 we have Paul's sufferings for Christ and the church plus the faithful ministry that claimed his pressing priority 24/7, as we might express it currently. "Christ in you, the hope of glory" are his immortal words in verse 27.

His committed and comprehensive ministry is depicted in verses 28-29. It was spiritual in breadth, length, depth and height as Paul expressed it so eloquently in Ephesians 3:18.

Colossians 1 is a monumental and magnificent chapter filled with golden nuggets of eternal truth.

HIGHLIGHTS FROM COLOSSIANS 2

In verses 1-2 we see exhibited Paul's sensitive concern for his esteemed brethren both at Colosse and Laodicea as well. Spiritual wishes are spelled out in Christ like concern. He knew how to pave the literary pathway for the refutation of the Colossian fallacy which permeates this entire chapter.

Verse 3 depicts just how much Christ should mean to them. They were heirs to spiritual wealth. Christ is all in all is a short summary of Paul's thinking.

In verses 4-8 we have weighty warnings and ardent admonitions extended. Perils are spelled out and solutions are inculcated for spiritual success.

In verses 9-11 the apostolic penman affirms all-sufficiency and absolute completion are in Christ. This refuted Gnosticism in thorough fashion.

In verses 12-13 baptism and conversion are shown to be in holy harmony. Baptism's action is revealed in clear fashion. Pictured here is a spiritual operation which they underwent in bonafide conversion.

Verses 14-17 make clear that Mosaic law has been blotted out or removed. Ephesians 2:15 and Hebrews 10:9 attest to the same—the removal of the old and the bringing in of the new. The shadow (Moses' system) is gone; the substance (Christ's system) remains. Some of our brethren have begun to tamper with this crystal clear passage denying its connection with Mosaic mandates being removed. They try to muddy a crystal clear stream.

Two primary thoughts permeate verses 18-22—do not be beguiled; stay glued or cemented to truth. The Colossian error is refuted in thorough fashion in these five power-packed verses.

Verse 23 reflects the grave dangers that come from will-worship. This is worship based on human will--not Divine will. Yet, will-worship dominates the mindsets of twenty-first century worshippers en masse. Such should not be, but alas it is!

HIGHLIGHTS OF CHAPTER 3

This chapter majors in Christian living. Romans 12 and Titus 2 are also great chapters on Christian living at its finest.

In verses 1-3 we have things above versus things below. Colossians 3:1 goes back to Colossians 2:12. They had been raised from their burial with Christ. In conversion there is a death to the love and practice of sin; there is a burial in water;

there is a rising there from. Ruled out wholly here are sprinkling, pouring and a recital of the so-called and deeply fatal sinner's bench prayer. The latter is the modern child of the old mourner's bench system. Relative to it someone once asked, "What is the difference between the mourner's bench and Acts 2:38?" The altogether appropriate response was, "One is from the sawmill and the other is from heaven." Surely, we do not have to spell out which is which! These modern salvation plans utterly fail in meeting the essentials set forth in Colossians 2:12 and 3-1. Why is the religious world so slow and sluggish in grasping such and adhering to that which is false to the very core? Such is amazingly amazing!

Verse 4 is one of more than 300 versus depicting Christ's second advent. If we are faithful and fervent, we shall "appear with him in glory." Paul was educating them in their need to be prepared for that good, great and grand day. It will be day of days for a surety.

In verses 4-9 Paul delineates the mortification process at work. Spelled out are evils and undesirables that need to be put to death. These war against the soul (Cf. 1 Pet. 2:11). Practice of such keeps the doors of hell wide open and the door of heaven tightly closed. Specified transgressions are of two kinds—sins of the flesh and sins of the disposition. Either group is fatal to souls.

With the negative set forth in verses 4-9 Paul follows with precious positives in verses 10-14. These are spiritual traits added to our changed lives. They will adorn us with spiritual beauty. This is the path of preparation for the Lord's second advent. This is a sure way to meet Him in peace.

Verse 15 informs us of our need to have a ruler over our hearts. It is to be the peace of God. We have been called (by the gospel) in one body. That one body is the church (Col. 1:18; Eph. 1:22-23). We are admonished to be thankful. He who thinks is going to be thankful. Look where this leaves the ingrate! Gratitude is a great adornment to the life of any saint of the most High God.

Verse 16 is a precious parallel to Ephesians 5:19. Together, they authorize singing in Christian worship minus any and all mechanical music in Christian worship. The authorized kind of songs is set forth.

Verse 17 is permeated and even overflows with the clear ring of supreme authority. In word and deed we are obligated to do all in the name (by His authority) of the Lord. Gratitude is linked again as it was in Colossians 3:15. Paul did not want them to forget how to be grateful. Many do not remember it very well in our day.

In verses 18-21 we have marital, parental and offspring obligations established. Paul did more of the same in a much more detailed account in Ephesians 5:22-33; 6:1-4.

Needed instructions for servants or slaves dominate verses 22-25. Shackles were not removed the moment slaves became Christians. They could be, and must be, Christ like while in shackles. In such roles they were serving Christ. Christian principles were being put into place to soften slavery and then eliminate it permanently. History proves that to have been the most prudent policy.

HIGHLIGHTS OF COLOSSIANS 4

Masters are addressed in verse 1. They were to be just and right in the treatment they gave their slaves. They are reminded of their own Heavenly Master. To Him they would one day give account.

In verses 2-4 prayers are emphasized. Paul desired their prayers for him, that open doors for evangelization, not Roman prison doors be opened, might be provided and that he might speak as duty demanded.

In verses 5-6 there is to be a worthy walk and wholesome speech patterns prevailing.

In verses 7-14 Paul lists by name eight of his fellow-laborers. He loved them and they loved him in return. It was not a case of unrequited love such as he experienced among the fickle Corinthians in 2 Corinthians 12:15.

In verses 15-18 we have closing admonitions both congregationally and individually. Paul addressed the many—not just the selected few. He concludes with grace and the final Amen.

CONCLUSION

People who love and respect Paul and this marvelous missive will never bash Christ or His church. Those who do are total strangers to Paul, the apostle and Paul, the Christian. Even more importantly, they are total strangers to God the Father, God the Son and God the Holy Spirit.

STUDY QUESTIONS

1. Give some historical background of Colosse.
2. Discuss the establishment of the Colossian congregation.
3. Discuss Colossians touching its author, date of writing, location where penned and the why of its composition.
4. What was the nature of the Colossian fallacy and why was it so fatal or lethal?
5. Discuss highlights from Colossians 1.
6. Discuss highlights from Colossians 2.
7. Discuss highlights from Colossians 3.
8. Discuss highlights from Colossians 4.
9. People who love God, Christ, Spirit, Paul and this epistle will never bash the church. Tell why.
10. Why is bashing the church such a lethal practice and why do you think it is growing at such an alarming rate?

WORKS CITED

All Scriptures are from the KJV unless otherwise noted.

The Churches of the New Testament: The Church at Sardis

INTRODUCTION

Sardis was some thirty miles east of Thyatira. It was one of the oldest, as well as one of the most important cities of Asia Minor. It was the capital of Lydia until the Persian king Cyrus took the city in 549 B. C. The city was built on a smooth, almost vertical rock hill on Mt. Tmolus, which was inaccessible from three sides. The fourth side was easily defended. With the river Pactolus serving somewhat as a moat at the base of the mountain, the city was virtually invincible.

The people of Sardis seemed to bask in the seeming impregnability of the city. However, history records two occasions in which the city was taken because the inhabitants of the city felt so secure in their natural defenses, they left the cliffs unguarded. Cyrus took the city in 549 B. C. and Antiochus the great likewise took the city unawares in 214 B. C.

Sardis was the glory of the Lydian empire, being one of the wealthiest cities of the entire world. Croesus was her most famous king. In fact, his name was connected to a famous proverb. When suggesting a person was exceedingly wealthy, they would say a person was "As rich as Croesus."

Religiously speaking, the city was noted for its temple dedicated to their patron deity, Cybele. The worship of Cybele was similar to the worship of Diana of Ephesus. Interestingly enough, a temple to Diana was begun in the city, but never completed.

The name of the person who first brought the gospel to this former wealthy city is shrouded in silence. It certainly could have been the apostle Paul, but to go beyond this is to enter into the realm of mere speculation.

Let us be content with one thing we do know: "The word of the truth of the gospel" (Col. 1:5) came to Sardis through the efforts of one who believed the gospel was for all men "For all have sinned, and come short of the glory of God" (Rom. 3:23).

Commentary

> And unto the angel of the church in Sardis write; These things saith he that hath the seven Spirits of God, and the seven stars; I know thy works, that thou hast a name that thou livest, and art dead (Rev. 3:1).

The words Jesus sent to the Christians in Sardis through John the apostle are indeed grave. The problem is simple: What everyone thought was the case, was in fact, not the true picture.

There is much speculation relative to the angel of the seven congregations. Total agreement of this issue will never be enjoyed this side of eternity. It is my judgment Wallace sets forth the most reasonable explanation, arguing the angel is the individual character of each congregation.1 Regardless of whether one agrees with this or not, everyone agrees the angel of each congregation named in the Revelation sustained a specific relationship with that specific congregation.

He that has "the seven Spirits of God and the seven stars" is Christ. The Lord said, "The seven stars are the angels of the seven churches: and the seven candlesticks which thou sawest are the seven churches" (Rev. 1:20). The "seven spirits of God" are explained as being "seven lamps of fire burning before the throne" (Rev. 4:5) and in Revelation 5:6, John states he saw a "lamb as it had been slain having seven horns and seven eyes which are the seven Spirits of God sent forth into all the earth." The lamb slain can only be Christ. The lamps, horns, and eyes come together to show the omnipresence and omniscience of the Lord. It is only by the all-seeing eye of Jehovah that could He say, "I know thy works, that thou hast a name that thou livest, and art dead." What is thought about a congregation is sometimes world's apart from that which the Lord sees. Everyone thought they were alive, but were near death. "Be watchful, and strengthen the things which remain, that are ready to die: for I have not found thy works perfect before God" (Rev. 3:2).

Jesus cautions for diligence in watchfulness because all was not dead. They were to strengthen the remaining things which "are ready to die."

The imperfect works alluded to here are incomplete works. The word translated "perfect" is rendered fulfil in more than half of its appearances in the New Testament. Thus, the works here contemplated had not been fulfilled.

> Remember therefore how thou hast received and heard, and hold fast, and repent. If therefore thou shalt not watch, I will come on thee as a thief, and thou shalt not know what hour I will come upon thee (Rev. 3:3).

Peter desired to put his readers in "remembrance" of certain things (2 Pet. 1:12-13; 1:15). If such was desired for those of whom Peter could say "though ye know them, and be established in the present truth," should the Lord not also desire those who were on the road to spiritual death do the same? The rich man remembered five brethren who would come to the same place of woe (Luke 16:28). Paul remembered his great opposition to the spread of the gospel (Acts 26:11). "Remember" should be a part of our very existence.

"How thou hast received" is most interesting. "How" is an adverb and refers to the manner in which they had received the Word of God. Had they manifested the "readiness of mind" of the Berean? Was it in the midst of severe persecution as at Thessalonica (Acts 17:1-9)? We cannot know with any degree of certainty. There is one thing certain that should not be overlooked: They heard the life saving gospel of Christ and obeyed it.

Emphasis is likewise given to what they heard. The pure gospel of Christ, undeniably confirmed by the miraculous, was to be the focus of their trip down "memory's lane." The greatest love story ever told was theirs. But they had slighted it, they had allowed their attention to wander and "I have not found thy works perfect before God." The remaining few things were about to die.

They were admonished to once again hold fast that from which they had strayed. In order to possess it, they must repent. Biblical repentance is a change of heart which issues in a changed life. They must turn back to the Lord or they will ultimately perish.

"Watch" in this verse implies preparedness. If they were not watchful and did not make the needed changes, the longsuffering of Christ would soon be exhausted. The things they would face are less than pleasing to contemplate. The exact time of His coming in judgment was not revealed, but that He would come if they failed to comply with His will was clearly stated. "Thou hast a few names even in Sardis which have not defiled their garments; and they shall walk with me in white: for they are worthy" (Rev. 3:4).

Here Paul's words come to mind when he wrote, "For God is not unrighteous to forget your work and labour of love, which ye have shewed toward his name, in that ye have ministered to the saints, and do minister" (Heb. 6:10). Just as the Lord never overlooks sin in our lives, so he never forgets righteousness in His people. Regardless of whether they are many or few in a congregation, God always looks favorably upon them.

"White" represents the "righteousness of the saints" (Rev. 19:8), and describes those walking in the truth. There is "no bed of roses" promised in this life, but those who look, listen, and heed "shall walk with me in white: for they are worthy."

Their works were found "perfect" before Him. They knew what the Lord required of them and they followed it with watchfulness. What they might be called upon to endure in this life is not stated here. However, there is that promise our faithfulness in this life will be rewarded, far beyond our ability to comprehend. Paul said it so well, "For I reckon that the sufferings of this present time are not worthy to be compared with the glory which shall be revealed in us" (Rom. 8:18).

> He that overcometh, the same shall be clothed in white raiment; and I will not blot out his name out of the book of life, but I will confess his name before my Father, and before his angels (Rev 3:5).

We must "overcome" in this life so we might "come over" and be with Him in eternity. Again the "righteousness of the saints" is pictured by the white raiment. Such victory would result in one's name remaining in the book of life. Jesus promised "I will confess his name before my Father, and before his angels."

Based upon Jesus' words "I will not blot out his name out of the book of life", some have affirmed this was one of the most difficult verses in the book of Revelation. We can understand their perplexity when we realize they believe in the denominational doctrine of The perseverance of the saints, that is, "once saved, always saved."

The words "Judas by transgression fell" (Acts 1:25) forever cry out against this doctrine of man. One of the original twelve apostles, hand-picked by Jesus Himself, did fall from God's favor. If one denies this, he denies inspiration. Paul stated what he did was done "lest that by any means, when I have preached to others, I myself should be a castaway" (1 Cor. 9:27). Judas fell--that much we can confidently affirm. There are two questions which must be raised: (1) From what did Judas fall, and (2) Into what did he fall?

If the Christians in Sardis could not fall, then Jesus' statement makes absolutely no sense at all. If those that overcome will have their names confessed before the Father, what will be the lot of those who did not overcome? Will they receive the same reward? "He that hath an ear, let him hear what the Spirit saith unto the churches" (Rev 3:6).

As in many other places, the word hear is used in the sense of to give heed to what is said. People need to pay attention to what the Lord has said. Often they hear the words, but do not give ear (heed) to what is said.

Anyone who hears the Lord's warnings and exhortations and ultimately overcomes, they will enjoy the promises and blessings here extended. Those who will not hear will one day stand before a righteous God and hear the words, "Depart from me ye that work iniquity, I never knew you" (Matt. 7:23).

OBSERVATIONS AND APPLICATIONS

One of the great challenges Sardis faced was "I have not found thy works perfect before God" (Rev. 3:2). The proper relationship between faith and works is as much a problem today as it was then. For all intents and purposes, members of the Lord's Church today do not fully understand the correlation between these two items.

Our denominational acquaintances and liberal brethren affirm anyone advocating baptism is essential for salvation is arguing for a "works salvation," and then quote "For by grace are ye saved through faith; and that not of yourselves: it is the gift of God: Not of works, lest any man should boast" (Eph. 2:8-9). Generally my brethren will fall all over themselves running backwards and apologizing. I affirm the person who says I believe in a works salvation is either ignorant (lack of knowledge) of what I teach or they are dishonest.

What our detractors must realize is the Bible clearly teaches there are two kinds of works. We cannot "work" so as to obligate God to save us. There is nothing we can do whereby we can stand before the Sovereign Ruler of the universe and say, "Pay me the salvation you owe me because of what I have done." This is not part or parcel of the gospel of Christ.

On the other hand, there are some "works" God demands of His children. Christians do these things, not to earn salvation (obligate God to save us), but because we are members of His spiritual body, the only institution through which God works.

Proof of the above remarks are easy to find. It is interesting the "salvation by faith only" people are quick to quote "For by grace are ye saved through faith; and that not of yourselves: it is the gift of God: Not of works, lest any man should boast" (Eph. 2:8-9). Every word in these two verses are there because the Holy Spirit wanted them included.

It is, however, most strange those who ever stand ready to quote these two verses so conveniently forget to read the very next verse. In verse ten, Paul penned the following words, "For we are his workmanship, created in Christ Jesus unto good works, which God hath before ordained that we should walk in them." Now, notice what some would say is a contradiction: In verse nine Paul said "not of works." But in verse ten he wrote we are created in Christ "unto good works," which God has ordained "we should walk in them."

Is there a contradiction? Of course not! There are two kinds of works. The "works" of verse nine are works of such a nature that God rewards them as a matter of debt, a payment in full of what He (God) owes man because man has earned it.

The "works" of verse ten are those "works" which issue from those redeemed by the blood of Christ. Christians realize they are a part of the New Testament Church, through which the Lord works. We do not work "to be saved," but work because we have been saved, because we have been added to the church (Acts 2:47).

CONSIDER ROMANS 4:3 AND JAMES 2:23

That there are two kinds of "works" is easily seen when one examines Romans 4:3 and James 2:23. Let us look closely at the following thoughts.

In a section of Scripture wherein Paul argues that Jew and Gentile alike need the gospel, he draws the Jewish mind to Abraham. He affirms that if Abraham "were justified by works, he hath whereof to glory, but not before God." In order to show Abraham was not justified by works, Paul wrote, "For what saith the scripture? Abraham believed God, and it was counted unto him for righteousness" (Rom. 4:3). The passage quoted is Genesis 15:6.

Let us look closely at the background of the passage Paul quoted. God had made a promise to Abram that "in thee shall all families of the earth be blessed" (Gen. 12:3). Some time later, this great Patriarch mentioned his childlessness and pointed to Eliezer of Damascus as his heir. God quickly informs Abram this was not the heir. God then"...brought him forth abroad, and said, Look now toward heaven, and tell the stars, if thou be able to number them: and he said unto him, So shall thy seed be" (Gen. 15:5). The Bible says of Abram, "And he believed in the LORD; and he counted it to him for righteousness" (Gen. 15:6). This is the very passage Paul quoted in Romans 4:3 to show justification is by faith.

It is worthy of notice James also quoted Genesis 15:6. He affirmed "Even so faith, if it hath not works, is dead, being alone" (Jam. 2:17)..."But wilt thou know, O vain man, that faith without works is dead?" (Jam. 2:20). He then mentions the incident of Abraham "when he had offered Isaac his son upon the altar' (Jam. 2:21). Now notice the next three verses which read,

Seest thou how faith wrought with his works, and by works was faith made perfect? And the scripture was fulfilled which saith, Abraham believed God, and it was imputed unto him for righteousness: and he was called the Friend of God. Ye see then how that by works a man is justified, and not by faith only (Jam. 2:22-24).

What we have now is two inspired writers quoting the same passage to prove what some people allege are contradictory positions. Paul used the passage to show man is justified by faith and not by works, while James quoted it to prove one is justified by works and not by faith only (Jam. 2:24). How can justification be "not by works" and "by works" at the same time?

The answer is amazingly simple if we understand James contemplated works which were totally different than those Paul had under consideration. The two inspired men were not writing about the same thing (works)! There is no contradiction here. In fact, there is absolute harmony between Paul and James.

FAITH MADE PERFECT BY WORKS

In the passages here considered, James made one of the more impressive statements found in the Bible. He wrote,
Seest thou how faith wrought with his works, and by works was faith made perfect? And the scripture was fulfilled which saith, Abraham believed God, and it was imputed unto him for righteousness: and he was called the Friend of God (Jam. 2:22-23).

Notice the affirmation, not only was Abraham's faith made perfect by works, but James affirmed Genesis 15:6 was fulfilled in the events of Genesis twenty two!

I would like to insert some thoughts penned by the wise and sagacious Guy N. Woods. He wrote:
23 and the scripture was fulfilled which saith, And Abraham believed God, and it was reckoned unto him for righteousness ;—The Scripture alluded to here is Gen. 15:6: "And he believed in Jehovah; and he reckoned it to him for righteousness." This was affirmed of Abraham after the illustrious patriarch had accepted,

without question, and despite his childlessness, and the advanced ages of himself and his wife Sarah, God's promise of vast posterity. Not knowing at the time how such could be, he nevertheless believed that it would be and stumbled not at the promise of God in unbelief. This scripture (Gen. 15:6), is declared to have been fulfilled when Abraham's faith was made perfect. It is vitally important to observe when the scripture referred to was fulfilled. Though Abraham was earlier (Gen. 15:6), acknowledged as a believer, and his faith "reckoned" for righteousness, it was not until later (Gen. 22:1-19), that his faith was consummated (made perfect) in the act of obedience involving Isaac. Abraham believed God, prior to this act of obedience; i.e., he fully accepted God's Word, and relied implicitly on the promises which it contained; and, as a result, his faith "was reckoned unto him for righteousness...." "To reckon," (elogisthe) is to regard, deem, consider, account; hence, God deemed, considered, regarded Abraham's faith as righteousness (right-doing). Faith itself, thus became an act of obedience which, in its exercise, and when, at the moment, there were no additional duties devolving upon Abraham. God accepted as proof of Abraham's devotion. One must not from this assume that the exercise of belief bestowed upon Abraham blessings apart from and independent of any obedience; though this conclusion is often drawn, it is an erroneous and hurtful one. In the nature of the case, the promise of great posterity involved matters which would require considerable time for their development; hence, there was nothing more, at the moment, for Abraham to do but to accept, without hesitation, the assurances of such from God. This, he did; and his acceptance thereof, became an act of righteousness which God, in his turn, accepted, and put to Abraham's account for righteousness (right-doing). It is a violent perversion of this passage and historic incident from it to assume that because Abraham's faith was accepted as an act of righteousness when there was nothing else required of him at the time that in our case faith will suffice without the performance of those conditions which are required of us now. Even in Abraham's case, as James so clearly shows, the patriarch's faith did not reach its consummation, its fulfillment, until it had translated itself into action in the offering of Isaac. 2

In my judgment, there is not much that can be added to this scholarly exposition of this passage. If I were to attempt to do so, it might only result in adding confusion and distraction to clarity and conciseness.

Just as the works of the Christians in Sardis were imperfect, so ours can also be in the twenty-first century. Just as Jesus found them lacking, so will He find us lacking if we mimic them. As He was displeased with them, so He will be disgusted with us also.

All saved comprise the New Testament Church, which in turn is His body (Eph. 1:22-23), the very instrument through which He works. If we are not about the Father's business (Luke 2:49), His business is left undone.

Let all of us be diligent relative to the Lord's business. We must keep in mind; Christians (individually and collectively) constitute that by which the Lord's work is done.

CONCLUSION

When people see the Biblical connection existing between faith and works, they understand works can never be construed as the performance of deeds which would obligate God to reward that person as payment of debt. There is not one thing man could do which would allow him to stand before God and affirm he has earned salvation.

Likewise, a proper understanding of faith and works makes one realize they have an obligation to make proper use of their time in God's service. We acknowledge the fact we are individual members of the New Testament Church, that one institution through which God works. If His will is done here upon earth, it will be members of the Church, either individually or collectively that do it.

Paul wrote, "For in Jesus Christ neither circumcision availeth any thing, nor uncircumcision; but faith which worketh by love" (Gal. 5:6). According to him, faith manifests itself by works. This is exactly what James said, "Even so faith, if it hath not works, is dead, being alone" (Jas. 2:17). Therefore, we see an instance in which Paul and James are using the word works exactly alike.

The faith of the Roman Christians was "spoken of throughout the whole world" (Rom. 1:8). Does anyone think for a moment the Church at Rome was sending out bulletins about their faith, telling everyone how faithful they were? Certainly not! They manifested their faith by their works. As James said, "Faith without works is dead" (Jam. 2:20).

Paul told the Colossian Christians he had heard of their faith. He wrote, "Since we heard of your faith in Christ Jesus, and of the love which ye have to all the saints" (Col. 1:4). How could he 'hear of their faith'? It is simple; he had heard what they were doing.

In the same context he wrote,

> For the hope which is laid up for you in heaven, whereof ye heard before in the word of the truth of the gospel; Which is come unto you, as it is in all the world; and bringeth forth fruit, as it doth also in you, since the day ye heard of it, and knew the grace of God in truth (Col. 1:5-6).

How does the word of God bring "forth fruit"? It is simple. God's Word is heard, taken into one's heart and obeyed. "For as the body without the spirit is dead, so faith without works is dead also" (Jas. 2:26).

Paul remembered how the Thessalonians manifested their faith. He wrote, "Remembering without ceasing your work of faith, and labour of love, and patience of hope in our Lord Jesus Christ, in the sight of God and our Father" (1 Thess. 1:3). Does anyone think for a moment the Thessalonian Christians just stood around, reminding Paul of their faith? Indeed, no! They believed the gospel message and manifested their faith by doing what God wanted them to do.

STUDY QUESTIONS

1. Which false god was the patron deity of Sardis?
2. What did the Christians in Sardis think about their works?
3. What did Christ think about their works?
4. What is the difference between works that are "ready to die" and works that are dead?
5. What does "white" represent in the book of Revelation?
6. What must one do so their name will not be blotted out of the book of life?
7. Why are the words "I will not blot out his name out of the book of life" so troubling to many denominational people?
8. What do the words "He that hath an ear, let him hear" really mean?
9. How can we say that salvation is not of works, but without works one cannot be saved?
10. Paul said the faith of the Roman Christians was "spoken of throughout the whole world" (Rom. 1:8).
    Please explain what he meant.

WORKS CITED

Foy E. Wallace, Jr., The Book of Revelation (Nashville, TN: Foy E. Wallace Jr. Publications, 1967), p. 83.

Guy N. Woods, A Commentary on the Epistle of James (Nashville TN: Gospel Advocate CO.,1967), pp.145-146.

The Church at Smyrna

The Churches OF THE New Testament

INTRODUCTION

To better understand the church at Smyrna, one would need to know a little about the city, the culture and the people of that area. The ancient city of Smyrna sat on the west coast of Asia Minor about thirty five miles north of Ephesus. It lay at the end of a major east west road, possessed an excellent harbor, and was surrounded by rich farm land. It sits on one of the most sheltered inlets of the Aegean Sea.1 Excavations by Ankara University have shown the primitive site was 13 km. (8 mi.) North East across the Kemer River, at the opposite edge of the bay, now Bayrakli-Tepekule. Pottery finds indicate the settlement was founded before 2000 B. C. and was Hittite (or a branch called 'Lelages' by Greek historians) until the immigration of Hellenic sea people connected with the fall of troy (ca. 1100). By John and Paul's day, Smyrna had become the highway terminus and commercial metropolis of an immensely fertile hinterland.2 As to the Culture, the ideals and thinking of the people probably goes back to their beginning, Polytheist. The Hittites, like their neighbors, adored many gods. Besides Set (or Sutekh), the "great ruler of heaven," and Ishtar (Ashtoreth), we also find mentioned (in Chattusil's treaty) gods and goddesses of "the hills and rivers of the land of the Chatti," "the great sea, the winds and the clouds." Tessupas was known to the Babylonians as a name of Rimmon, the god of thunder and rain. On a bilingual seal (in Hittite and cuneiform characters), now in the Ashmolean Museum, we noticed the goddess Ischara, whose name was equivalent to Istar among the Kassites. The Hittite gods are represented—like those of the Assyrians—standing erect on lions. One of them (at Samala in Syria) is lion-headed like Nergal.

They also believed in demons, like the Akkadians and others.3 As to the people, by the time of the writing of the book of Revelation, they were mostly Greek and Jews. It is said the Greek poet Homer was born there. By the time of the writing of the book of Revelation, the city was mostly Jewish. It is also said during this time Domitian was emperor of Rome and had instituted a persecution against Christians.

THE AUTHOR OF THE LETTER

It is very evident the author of this letter to the church at Smyrna knew from a personal perspective what these brethren were going through and what they were facing. He could speak about the victory one gains from being "faithful unto death" (Rev. 2:10), because he had been there (John 19:30; Lk. 22:42; Mk. 16:1ff). He could speak about being "...cast into prison and tried ten days..." because he had been there (Matt. 26:44-ff). He could speak about "...the blasphemy of those who say they are Jews and are not..." (Matt. 26:21, 45-50). Who better to write to this church about these things than Jesus Christ? This is the one John saw and described in chapter one of the book of Revelation who gave him the instructions to write the letter and send it to this church (Rev. 1:10-20; 2:8). Certainly, He knows about overcoming suffering and death through faith in God (Heb. 4:15; 5:8-9).

THE MESSAGE

I know that you are poor, but yet ye are rich.
They were poor from a human standpoint because they were going through tribulation and poverty, being blasphemed and killed. This resulted in many deaths. The folly of it is there was more to come! One writer put it this way; "...in A.D. 33, in consideration of Smyrna's long record of loyalty, it was the one chosen from the eleven cities contending for the privilege of building a temple to the emperor Agustus and his mother" (Tacitus Ann. lv. 56: C. Cadoux, Ancient Smyrna [1938]). It is clear why the Jews of Smyrna, more than those of neighboring towns, felt antagonism towards the Christians there.4

Also, if one would look at the date of the writing of this letter, (with respect to the persecution these Christians are said to be facing) he would better understand just how poor they were physically. Domitian was emperor of Rome at this time. It is said he instituted a persecution against Christians that was short (ca. 95 to 96 A.D.) but was extremely violent. Many Christians (thousands) are said to have been slain in Rome and Italy and many banished to Patmos.5 John the apostle was among those who were banished to Patmos (Rev. 1:9). Many who disagree with this date. They say it had to be earlier around c. 60-70 because when Jerusalem was mentioned (Rev. 11:1), there is no mention of its fall which happened in A.D. 70. The number "666" in Revelation 13:18 is said to be Nero Caesar who was emperor of Rome long before Domitian and created far more suffering and death for Christians than did he. Also, the listing of five kings in Revelation 17:9-11 is said to point with accuracy the date of the book. I believe the latter date to be very accurate because of the condition of the churches mentioned in this letter. Ephesus had left her first love; Sardis was said to be dead; Laodicea is lukewarm. This city appears to be a prosperous city in this book, yet in A.D. 62, during Nero's reign, it was destroyed by an earthquake. This letter, written to the church at Smyrna in the book of Revelation, definitely represents the historical circumstances of Domition's day and reign.

One of the most disturbing things we learn in this letter is about false brethren. You know the kind those which come into a congregation acting like a sheep but are nothing more than a wolf in sheep's clothing (Matt. 7:15). Peter calls them "spots" and says they have "forsaken the right way and are gone astray" (2 Pet. 2:13-ff). Jude says "these are spots in your feasts of charity" (Jude 12). Paul says to Titus they are nothing more than "unruly and vain talkers and deceivers" (Tit. 1:10). Paul said concerning the truth these have erred and in so doing they overthrow the faith of some (2 Tim. 2:17).

He says to the elders of the church at Ephesus they are grievous wolves (Acts 20:29). Also, he says these kinds only serve their own belly, and they use good words and fair speeches to deceive the hearts of the simple (Rom. 16:18). Their only desire is to steal, to kill, and to destroy (John 10:10). This is certainly evident in this letter because the church is told how they would be "blasphemed" and how they would be cast into prison and be tried and would have tribulation ten days (Rev. 2:9-10). If you had to go through this kind of persecution, how would you endure?

The Lord said suffering was a part of the Christian's life (Matt. 20:23). Paul said "all that will live godly in Christ Jesus shall suffer persecution" (2 Tim. 3:12). Peter said "But and if ye suffer for righteousness' sake, happy are ye" (1 Pet. 3:14). It is an undeniable fact that all men go through some kind of suffering, but not all are rewarded of God. This is why Peter said "But let none of you suffer as a murderer, or as a thief, or as an evildoer, or as a busybody in other men's matters. Yet if any man suffer as a Christian, let him not be ashamed; but let him glorify God on this behalf" (1 Pet. 4:15). All these saints had to do was be faithful (live righteously), and God would reward and not forsake them (Psa. 37:25). Even though they would have tribulation an equal number of days, if they would just stay faithful unto the end, the second death would not touch them (Rev. 2:11).

They were rich from a spiritual standpoint in that they were faithful and encouraged to remain so unto death (Rev. 2:10). It can be said of these Christians they "loved not their lives unto the death" (Rev. 12:11). This church was not like Ephesus who left their first love (Rev. 2:4), not like Laodicea lukewarm (Rev. 3:16), and unlike Sardis, really, really dead (Rev. 3:1). They were not like the church at Thyatira who allowed women preachers (Rev. 2:20). God does not allow women to usurp authority over the man [KJV], to have dominion over a man, [ASV] but to be in silence (1 Tim. 2:12). No, the church at Smyrna was rich in good works (Rev. 2:9).

CONCLUSION

As a result of the faithful works of this church, Jesus makes a promise unto them that all of humanity should want "He that overcometh shall not be hurt of the second death" (Rev. 2:11). The second death is described as a lake of fire (Rev. 20:14). It is also described as the lake which burneth with fire and brimstone (Rev. 21:8). All who live a sinful life are going to be cast into it (Rev. 21:8). To overcome means "to conquer, to carry off the victory, come off victorious, etc...". It is to do as Jesus Christ our Lord did, to gain the victory over his enemies; death, hell and the grave (1 Cor. 15:55). Jesus offered this victory to Smyrna then, and to us today if we are faithful unto death (1 Cor. 15:57) --"But thanks be to God, which giveth us the victory through our Lord Jesus Christ."

STUDY QUESTIONS

1. Where was Smyrna located?
2. Who authored the letter to the church?
3. What proof can be offered that Jesus was the author?
4. What type of church was this?
5. What was going to happen to the Christians at Smyrna if they did not repent?
6. How could one describe the poor state of this church?
7. How could one describe the rich state of this church?
8. What was promised to those who remained faithful unto death?
9. How long would they suffer tribulation?
10. By whom were they blasphemed?

WORKS CITED

Harpers Bible Dictionary, Pub. Harper and Row; yr. 1985, pgs. 960-961

International Standerard Bible Encyclopedia, Pub. Eerdmans; Yr. 1988, pg. 555

International Standerard Bible Encyclopedia, Pub. Eerdmans; Yr. 1988, pg. 556

Bible Knowledge Commentary, Pub. John F. Walvoord; Roy B. Zuck; Yr. 1983 Pg. 934

Halley's Bible Handbook, New Revised Ed., Pub. Zondervan, Yr. 1965, Pg. 761

The Church at Thessalonica

The Churches OF THE New Testament

INTRODUCTION

EARLY LIFE OF SAUL, THE PERSECUTOR

The great apostle Paul is the author of First and Second Thessalonians and thus identifies himself in the first epistle (1:1; 2:18) and in the second (1:1). From the steps of the Castle of Antonia when rescued from the mob by the chief captain in the temple area in Jerusalem, Paul stated, "I am a Jew, of Tarsus in Cilicia [a Roman province in Asia Minor], a citizen of no mean [average] city" (Acts 21:39). He further stated he was, born in Tarsus of Cilicia, but brought up in this city, at the feet of Gamaliel [in Jerusalem], instructed according to the strict manner of the law of our fathers, being zealous for God, even as ye all are this day: and I persecuted this way [cf. John 14:6] unto the death, binding and delivering into prisons both men and women (Acts 22:3-4).

Paul was a Roman born citizen (Acts 22:22-29). Further, he stated "I am a Pharisee, a son of Pharisees" (Acts 23:6). He was a severe persecutor of the church of Christ, even trying to get Christians to blaspheme and giving his vote that they be put to death (Acts 26:9-11); "in times past in the Jews' religion," Paul said that he had "beyond measure...persecuted the church of God, and made havoc of it: and I advanced in the Jews' religion beyond many of mine own countrymen, being exceedingly zealous for the traditions of my fathers" (Gal. 1:13-14).

The early life of Saul of Tarsus was greatly influenced by both Jewish revelation and Grecian philosophy, as would be expected by the location of Cilicia [between Palestine and Greece]. Tarsus, being no average city, was a rival in learning to Alexandria, Egypt. The young Saul would have received schooling in the Rabbinical school there [probably within or hard fast to the synagogue]. He was also very familiar with the Grecian poets and with Grecian thought (Acts 17:16-31).

Likely at age twelve, when he became a "son of the law," from his youth, Saul was sent to Jerusalem to study at the feet of Gamaliel, a Pharisee and a doctor of the law (Acts 5:34). Saul's formal education was enviable—far superior to that of most of his fellows. He was a deeply devout, very prejudiced Pharisee, living "before God in all good conscience until this day" (Acts 23:1). It is very possible that Saul returned [after his academic study] to Tarsus, where he may have served as "Rabbi." At any rate, he advanced far beyond his fellow Pharisees.

When the Lord's church was exceedingly multiplying in number in Jerusalem and "a great company of the priests [of the Jews] were obedient to the faith" (Acts 6:7), for whom would the Jewish leaders call to help quell such growth by the cause of Christ? Would they not seek their champion? All of the Jews far and wide knew of his tremendous zeal for the Pharisee sect (Acts 26:4-5), Indeed, possibly the one most rigorously "disputing with Stephen" among the various synagogues was this young Cilician (Acts 6:9). The first specific mention of Saul was at the stoning of Stephen, where he showed his endorsement of this vicious act; "the witnesses laid down their garments at the feet of a young man named Saul" (Acts 7:58). In fact, the record explicitly states, "And Saul was consenting unto his death" (Acts 8:1). The record further states that "on that day a great persecution [arose] against the church which was in Jerusalem; and they were all scattered abroad throughout the regions of Judaea and Samaria, except the apostles. And devout men buried Stephen, and made great lamentation over him. But Saul laid waste the church, entering into every house, and dragging men and women committed them to prison" (Acts 8:1-3).

CONVERSION AND EARLY PREACHING OF PAUL, THE APOSTLE

While the gospel was making its way to Samaria and beyond, Saul was "yet breathing threatening and slaughter against the disciples of the Lord" (Acts 9:1). Paul's having asked for and received letters to Damascus, from the high priest, authorizing him to arrest Christians and bring them to Jerusalem to be persecuted and/or killed (Acts 9:1-2). Christ appeared to Saul and asked, "Saul, Saul, why persecutest thou me?" (Acts 9:4). Christ appeared to and spoke to Saul personally, "to appoint thee a minister and a witness both of the things wherein thou hast seen me, and of the things wherein I will appear unto thee" (Acts 26:16), qualifying him to be a witness, to become an apostle of Christ, one "born out of due season" (Acts 22:14; Rom. 1:1; Acts 1:22). Upon Saul's being instructed by the Lord to go to Damascus where "it shall be told thee what thou must do" (Acts 9:6) and upon his being instructed by the preacher Ananias to "arise, and be baptized, and wash away thy sins, calling upon his name" (Acts 22:16), he thus obeyed. He became a Christian and was added to the church, which he had viciously, vigorously persecuted (cf. Acts 2:36-41,47). He immediately became Saul the preacher and himself the persecuted (Acts 26:20; 22:19-25). What a work Paul did for the Lord and to His glory; Paul "turned the world upside down."

Some time after the gospel had gone to the Gentiles, Saul [now called Paul] and Barnabas were sent forth by a Gentile church, Antioch, on Paul's first missionary journey (Acts 13-14). Some Jews and many Gentiles, especially God-fearers, obeyed the gospel, and numerous churches were established in Asia Minor. After the Jerusalem meeting, recorded in Acts 15 [A.D. 50], Paul and Silas departed on Paul's second missionary journey (Acts 15:40-41). [Incidentally, Galatians 2:1-3 reveals that Titus was taken by Paul to Jerusalem for the meeting of Acts 15; being a Greek, Titus was not compelled to be circumcised. He was one of Paul's beloved companions].

Having confirmed the churches in Syria and Cilicia, they came to Lystra, where Paul met Timothy, a Jew-Greek. Wanting to take Timothy with them, Paul had him circumcised, to allay possible criticism by the Jews. As they passed through Asia Minor, at Troas, Paul received a vision of a "man of Macedonia standing, beseeching, and saying, Come over into Macedonia, and help us." Luke joined their company, and they set sail for Europe, arriving at Philippi, in Northeast Greece about ten miles inland from the Aegean Sea. Because there was not sufficient Jewish heads of families [ten in number] to build a synagogue, Paul and his company went down to the river supposing that if there any worshippers of God in the city, they would likely, on the Sabbath, worship there [because of the Jewish washings involved]. Finding and teaching Lydia and her household, the gospel preachers baptized them (Acts 16:1-15).

Also in Philippi, Paul cast a demon out of a soothsaying maiden, not wishing that Satan have any involvement as they preached the gospel (Acts 16:16-18). Because the maiden's masters were deprived of their financial gain from her, they falsely accused Paul and Silas and had them beaten with "many stripes," thrown into the inner dungeon, and placed in very painful stocks. The resulting miracle and the worship to God by Paul and Silas led to the opportunity of teaching the jailor and his household, and they were baptized for the remission of sins and rejoiced greatly (Acts 16:19-40). Thus began the Lord's church in Philippi, in much affliction.

THE CITY OF THESSALONICA

Thessalonica was a very important city on the Egnatian Way ["Via Egnatia"], one of the most famous of the military roads of Rome. ["All roads led to Rome, but all roads led out of Rome, also. It was on these roads that the Gospel made its way throughout the Roman Empire."]. The Egnatian Way ran east and west and made vital connections with the great commercial seaport at Thessalonica [which was located some one hundred miles from Philippi] and with all points north and east of the city.

Such commerce brought many Jews and Greeks to this thriving metropolis. [Incidentally, the Jews, who were not as numerous in Thessalonica as the Greeks, Romans, and Orientals, had exerted quite an influence upon the religious thought of numerous former pagans, to the point of leading them to become believers in God, to learn the Old Testament Scriptures, and to attend the synagogue worship]. It also served at times as headquarters for Roman operations in Macedonia and beyond, such as during the time of Pompei. Earlier called Therma because of the hot springs on the site, the city was founded upon the ancient site by Cassander [a former officer in the army of Alexander the Great] in 315 B. C. It most likely derived its name from Cassander's wife, Thessalonica; she was a daughter of Phillip of Macedon and sister of Alexander the Great.

Thessalonica, because of its loyalty to Rome, was honored by Caesar Augustus [great emperor of Rome] when he made it a "free city." This meant the city could govern its own affairs in many areas internally. They were permitted to select their own "politarchs," or magistrates.

Being the second congregation established by the courageous apostle and his company in Europe, the gospel would sound forth and the Thessalonian church would be a potent force for Christianity's spread in Macedonia, Achaia, and beyond. The present-day city is called Solonica.

THE GOSPEL GOES TO THESSALONICA

Inasmuch as the synagogue [which was begun by the Jews in Babylon] was a "launching pad" for the preaching of the Good News of Christ, where there was a synagogue, Paul took opportunity to preach to the Jews and to the God-fearing Gentiles. In that there was a synagogue in Thessalonica, he reasoned with the Jews and the God-fearers in the synagogue for three Sabbath days, giving powerful evidence and argumentation that Jesus is the Christ, the resurrected Son of God, the fulfillment of Old Testament prophecy (Acts 17:1-3).

The short time Paul was in Thessalonica, he supported himself financially, working night and day making tents (1 Thess. 2:9; 2 Thess. 3:8), with additional help from the brethren at Philippi (Phi. 4:16). He did not wish to be a burden to anyone, and he certainly did not want to be identified with false religionists who went about with deceptive, selfish, ungodly motives. The response to the preaching of the gospel was that some Jews, a great multitude of the God-fearing Gentiles, and numerous chief women obeyed the truth. The result was the rabble-rousing Jews stirred up a mob mentality and violence, assaulting brother Jason, his household of Christians, and other brethren; they dragged them before the authorities and accused the brethren of "turning the world upside down" and of acting contrary to Caesar and of being traitors of Rome—a vicious false charge. When Jason and the other brethren paid a bond, they were released. "And the brethren immediately sent away Paul and Silas by night into Beroea" (Acts 17:4-10). If Paul was in Thessalonica for just the three Sabbath days mentioned above, then he was there for some fifteen to twenty-seven days.

Silas and Timothy remained in Beroea longer than Paul. After many obeyed the gospel there, the same radical Jews of Thessalonica came to Beroea and stirred up opposition to the young congregation, and Paul was sent away to Athens. While waiting for his sons in the gospel, Paul preached from the Areopagus, having reasoned with the Jews and devout Greeks in the synagogue and the marketplace. He disputed with the Epicurean and Stoic philosophers and delivered his profound sermon there on Mars Hill. He spoke of the only true and living God and of the living, resurrected Christ who shall judge the world. Some mocked, and others "clave to him." He then departed to Corinth, from which place he wrote First and Second Thessalonians (about 51-52 A.D.), First Thessalonians being the first epistle he wrote. Paul had sent Timothy back to Thessalonica "to establish you and to comfort you" and to "know your faith" (1 Thess. 3:1-5); Timothy brought Paul "good tidings," and they were comforted about the brethren in Thessalonica (1 Thess. 3:6-10).

PAUL'S EPISTLES TO THE THESSALONIANS

Having been unable to preach for very long in the city of Thessalonica, the apostle Paul must have been very concerned for the new converts and for the newly established congregation. Would they be able to endure; would his sudden departure result in their possible discouragement and abandonment of the faith; would they succumb to the pressures and temptations of their old pagan immorality or of Judaism; would they bow to the ridicule of their kinfolk and former friends; would they be overwhelmed spiritually by the persecutions of the powers that be (Acts 17:5-9)? Had they been sufficiently grounded to overcome the world and to persist in their faithful, devoted service to God? Paul was keenly aware of their immaturity and was very concerned for their welfare, as he was concerning all Christians. Dangers always abound; consequently, Paul wrote the Corinthians thus: "Besides those things that are without, there is that which presseth upon me daily, anxiety for all the churches" (2 Cor. 11:28). That anxiety would certainly include his sensitive care for the young church at Thessalonica.

It is therefore easy to visualize Paul's ease of mind, his relief, when Timothy brought good news about the new Christians:

> But when Timothy came even now unto us from you, and brought us glad tidings of your faith and love, and that ye have good remembrance of us always, longing to see us, even as we also to see you; for this cause, brethren, we were comforted over you in all our distress and affliction through your faith: for now we live, if ye stand fast in the Lord (1 Thess. 3:6-8).

He was so grateful and excited to hear the good report from Timothy that he wanted to express his joy by letter and to encourage them as follows: "Finally then, brethren, we beseech and exhort you in the Lord Jesus, that, as ye received of us how ye ought to walk and do walk,—that ye abound more and more" (4:1).

The Church At Thessalonica

Paul had sent Timothy back to Thessalonica from Athens "...to establish you and to comfort you concerning your faith; that no man be moved by these afflictions; for yourselves know that hereunto we are appointed. For verily, when we were with you, we told you before-hand that we are to suffer affliction; even as it came to pass, and ye know (3:1-4).

The tempter, Satan, was [and is] a real and present danger (1 Pet. 5:8); they [and we] must beware of his subtlety (cf. Gen. 3:1; 2 Cor. 11:3), "lest by any means the tempter had tempted you, and our labor should be in vain," Paul stated (1 Thess. 3:5). Paul continually gave thanks to God and prayed for the brethren (1:2-4). He was very thankful that they not only were imitators of Paul [and thus of Christ (1 Cor. 11:1)] but also that they had also sounded forth [and were themselves examples of] the truth in Macedonia and Achaia, and in every place (1 Thess. 1:5-8). Brethren in other cities and regions knew the Thessalonians had "turned unto God from idols, to serve a living and true God" (1:9). They had indeed, "when ye received from us the word of the message, even the word of God...accepted it not as the word of men, but, as it is in truth, the word of God, which worketh in you that believe" (2:13); Paul was thankful for that.

Whereas Paul rejoiced in the above good report regarding the Thessalonians, regretfully there was also some bad news. A first problem was that some enemies of the truth [even some members of the church, likely] were endeavoring to undermine the apostle Paul's character, influence, motives, and effectiveness in the kingdom [as is so often the case when brethren are having a positive effect in this old wicked world]. The apostle had brought to them the Gospel, which they had obeyed; he had given them great assurance, comfort, and hope in the Lord, both now and hereafter. Paul learned the opponents of truth had tried to discredit him and his message and to take away their comfort. Paul made it clear his motive was pure, and he sought to please God, not men. He had not used deception or flattery, but was as gentle as a nurse with her own children and as a father with his own children. He had even worked with his own hands, so as not to burden them. They knew his every area of conduct and deportment was holy, righteous, and blameless (2:2-12).

A second problem was they were confused relative to the future of those fellow brethren who had "fallen asleep"; those family and friends in the Lord had also obeyed the Gospel and had persevered in the face of great ridicule and persecution, but they had died. Thinking the Lord's second appearing was immediately to take place, they had deep concern that their dearly departed brothers and sisters in Christ would miss seeing Him and miss being blessed to go to heaven. Paul wrote to comfort them and to correct them relative to this lack of understanding. At the Lord's appearing, Paul wrote, the righteous, disembodied spirits [whom Christ will bring with Him] shall be reunited with their bodies in the graves and be raised from the dead, thus together with the righteous living meet the Lord in the air (4:13-18). He shall return as a thief in the night (5:1-11; cf. Mat. 24:36). He assured them there would be "the falling away first," before the Lord's personal return (2 Thess. 2:1-5).

A third problem was that some, thinking that Christ's return was immediate, stopped working at their jobs. They reasoned, why work when time is so short, and why work for those material things which are so soon to perish (1 Thess. 4:11)? Thus having too much time on their hands, they were living lives which were disorderly and were guilty of being busybodies, disrupting the peace of the congregation. Unless they repented, reformed their lives, and returned to work with quietness and to Peat their own bread, they were to be disciplined—the brethren were to withhold their fellowship from the disorderly, yet not treat them as enemies (2 Thess. 3:6-15).

A fourth problem was that they could fail to break completely with heathen depravity and immorality, characteristic of Satan's idolatrous, wicked kingdom from which they had been translated into the kingdom of light (1 Thess. 4:1-8; cf. Col. 1:13-14; 2 Pet. 2:20-22). Their false thinking that Christ's return was imminent could even encourage such ungodly, immoral conduct, rather than demonstrating love for each other in the peaceable kingdom (1 Thess. 4:9-12).

CONCLUSION

Paul was very grateful for the growth of the brethren in Thessalonica; he prayed for them and asked them to remember him and his fellow workers in their prayers. They were urged to continue in the inspired traditions [the Word of God] (2 Thess. 2:15), to reject spurious letters as if from Paul (2:2), and to admonish and encourage the weak (1 Thess. 5:14). He gave them assurance they would be blessed with eternal rest when Jesus returns, whereas their persecutors would suffer everlasting destruction (2 Thess. 1:6-10).

STUDY QUESTIONS

1. Paul studied under the feet of who?
2. The early life of Paul (Saul of Tarsus) was greatly influenced by what two things?
3. We first learn of Saul at what event?
4. Paul said that he was an apostle of Christ born out of what?
5. Who instructed Saul to be baptized?
6. Paul and Silas were beaten with many stripes in what city?
7. Thessalonica was the first or second congregation established by Paul?
8. Who brought news to Paul about the congregation in Thessalonica?
9. Did Paul receive any bad news about the church in Thessalonica?
10. One of the problems that the church in Thessalonica was having problems with was about the future of some who had already done what?

The Churches of The New Testament
The Church at Thyatira

INTRODUCTION

The beginning of the Lord's letters to the seven churches of Asia starts in this second great chapter of the book of Revelation. The letter written to the church at Thyatira is the longest of the seven letters. The book of Revelation has been the hotbed of speculation and every wild theory of man, mainly because of the apocalyptic style. This style was usually produced in times of persecution and oppression as a means of encouraging those who were suffering for their faith. This is exactly what was taking place as John penned the words to this letter. Let us consider the background and context of this letter.

To unify the Roman Empire, its emperor, Domitian, tried to create a single religion for all. To do so, he revived August Caesar's Imperial cult, declared himself "Lord God" and demanded all should pay him homage, even if they believed in other gods. Christians found this to be unacceptable (1 Cor. 8:6). Because of their non-compliance, they were targeted for persecution. During these difficult times, John received his vision of Jesus walking in the midst of seven lampstands, symbolic of seven churches in a world of chaos and crisis. To each He dedicated a letter of encouragement and outlined areas in which they needed to change if they were to remain loyal members of His church. With this background in mind, let us examine the church at Thyatira.

Thyatira was a great trading city and center of communication, with many people coming and going. It was situated in a valley that connected two other valleys and located southeast of Pergamos. It had no natural fortification at all and although at this time the Roman garrison was stationed there, their aim was not to defend Thyatira, but to delay the invaders long enough for Pergamum, the capital nearby, to be prepared for the coming attack. Thyatira was dispensable in the economy of the day.

We also know from history Thyatira was very industrial. It was home to tanners, potters, wool workers, makers of various kinds of linen apparel, dyes, etc. These various industries and trades were linked with the worship of other gods. Each guild had its particular guardian god. As a member, you would be expected to attend all its functions and participate in its activities which included offerings, feast and often immoral behavior. Because of this, the members of the Lord's church were torn between making a living, which meant participating in these activities, and staying faithful to Christ and His standards. It was from this city and environment that Lydia, a business lady, a seller of purple, who was in Philippi, a colony of Macedonia about three hundred miles from Thyatira was converted to Christ (Acts 16:14-15).

Thyatira had no special significance religiously. It was not a center of Caesar worship like Pergamum, nor of Greek worship like Ephesus. The two notable things about the city from a religious perspective was it had a local god by the name of Tyrimnus. His image was on their coins, and it possessed a fortune-telling shrine presided over by a female oracle called the Sambathe. Religious persecution was not necessarily an issue in Thyatira; however, there was a type of economic persecution that came as a result of the trade guilds. These guilds represented different trades in the city, but they were much more than that. The guilds operated such as service clubs do today, so their influence in the community was substantial.

The guilds often held common meals, which more often than not happened in the temple and would begin and end with a formal sacrifice to the various gods. The meat served during the meals would have been meat offered to one god or another. If that was not bad enough, the meals often became an excuse for excess and often degenerated into immorality.

So the question was: Should the Christian be involved in the guilds when their involvement would include, at the very minimum, attendance at these events? The other option for the Christian was not to be involved or belong to a guild. However, due to the far reaching influence of these organizations, this option would virtually guarantee economic ruin and commercial collapse.

This study begins by Jesus introducing Himself. The description is very plain and simple. Verse 18 states this message was from the Son of God, whose eyes are bright like flames of fire, whose feet are like fine or polished brass. Most commentators agree this describes two of Jesus' attributes--that He is all seeing and all powerful. With this introduction, He is about to commend and condemn the church at Thyatira.

With this background and context information in mind, let us now consider the letter as a whole.

APPRECIATION

Jesus begins this letter, as He does in all but one of His letters, with praise and appreciation. In this case He says, "I know thy works, and charity, and service, and faith, and thy patience, and thy works..." (Rev. 2:19). From this commendation we notice none of these traits are passive; they are all active and all positive. Jesus begins with these words, "I know thy works..." We must realize Jesus knows everything we do. Christianity is a religion of action. We are commanded not to be hearers of God's Word only, but also doers of His word (James 1:22). In the great Sermon on the Mount, Jesus taught, "Not everyone that saith unto me, Lord, Lord, shall enter into the kingdom of heaven; but he that doeth the will of my Father which is in heaven" (Matt. 7:21). In Revelation 2:23, Jesus stated, "I am he that searcheth the reins and hearts, and will give every one of you according to your works". Then, Jesus begins to tell them what it is He knows about the church at Thyatira. It is interesting that three of the four qualities mentioned here are all listed as fruit of the Spirit in Galatians 5:22-23. Let us notice these positive traits:

Charity – the love mentioned here is not some "wishy-washy" type of love often spoken of in today's media. This is not the word that can be used of anything from loving fried chicken or pizza to the undying love of a spouse or child. Instead this is an Agape love, an all-giving, non-demanding love--a love that loves regardless of what is in it for me. All they did seems to be motivated by love. They loved the saint, the sinner and the Savior. This love motivated them to work. When we love as we should, we will work as we should.

The Church At Thyatira

Service – this word service means anything done voluntarily out of love and concern for someone in need. The word "service" comes from the Greek word "diakonia" meaning "ministry". It is descriptive of giving attendance to certain needs. This is the same type of service that James the brother of Jesus speaks of in James 2:15-16. Suppose you see a brother or sister who needs food or clothing, and you say, "good-bye and God bless you, stay warm and eat well". Then, you do not give that person any food or clothing. What good does that do? This congregation had the attitude of serving one another and serving others.

Faith – this faith is not just a believing faith but a faithfulness, a faith that overcomes and is the highest form of loyalty. This is the kind of faith that says, "I may not understand, but that's ok." The Hebrew writer stated, "without faith it is impossible to please God" (Heb. 11:6). Faith is a five letter word that is easy to say but often hard to live. We understand and know an enduring faith is essential to our salvation. It is a deep abiding confidence in God rather than oneself. Our faith is such an important part of our walk with God and our faith comes by hearing the Word of God (Rom. 10:17).

Patience – this endurance comes from the faith that God is in control and is coming again. Do we fully understand what it is we are awaiting? The book of Revelation is filled with promises, but unless you read the book, you will not know what the promises are. You will just be waiting in a vague sense. The story of the book of Revelation is Jesus is coming back and the children of God, who have waited and remained faithful, will overcome and be victorious.

Works – this word was used as a general reference to their manner of life. This word was used to bring out the fact that they performed good deeds for the welfare of others.

Growth (and the last to be more than the first) – remember the church in Ephesus was criticized for leaving their first love. I am often amazed at the initial response of an individual who responds to the Lord's invitation and obeys the Gospel. They are often full of enthusiasm. As time goes by, they cool down, and often lose their first love.

This was not the case with those at Thyatira. They just kept getting better and better and continued to grow. Christianity is not supposed to be stagnant; it is supposed to be vibrant and exciting (2 Pet. 3:18).

At this time, the church must have been feeling pretty good about themselves. Jesus seems pretty pleased with them until we read the word "Notwithstanding". The newer translations use the word "but" and after the "but" comes the truth. This word is a transitional word. With the transition the next words are not always positive or pleasant; they can bring both good or bad news.

ACCUSATIONS

Jesus states in verse 20-21 – "Notwithstanding, I have a few things against thee..." You are permitting that woman, Jezebel who calls herself a prophet, to lead my servants astray. She is encouraging them to worship idols, eat food offered to idols, and commit sexual sin. I gave her time to repent, but she would not turn away from her immorality. When Jesus called this woman "Jezebel", it was a description rather than identification. Jesus was describing her nature rather than giving her name.

In the book of 1 Kings we read of a woman named Jezebel who married Ahab. Ahab was the king of Israel when he married Jezebel the daughter of Ethbaal king of the Sidonians. Ahab began to serve Baal and worship him. He set up an altar for Baal in the temple of Baal that he built in Samaria. This angered God and he punished both Ahab and Jezebel. Jezebel was, without a doubt, one of the most wicked women in the Bible. This woman at Thyatira apparently was an evil and wicked woman.

Just as Jezebel influenced Ahab to sin against God, this woman in the church at Thyatira was influencing members of the Lord's church. By her teachings, she misled many into sexual immorality. There are those today who profess to be Christians that try to alter the teachings of the Bible to fit their lifestyle or beliefs. According to the Bible, these people should be removed from the church if they refuse to change.

The Greek word used here for sexual immorality is "proneuo". This is the same word from which we get our word pornography. "Proneuo" means to engage in unlawful lust or sex. Isn't it amazing that in our society and even within the church we are going through the same thing thousands of years later? Recently the US Supreme Court ruled a picture on the Internet that has been altered to look like adults are having sex with children is legal. How can anyone believe this is acceptable? Many Christians today including preachers, elders and deacons are addicted to Internet pornography and some are even committing acts of fornication. How sad it is that the church at Thyatira was allowing this woman to teach and have such an influence. In verse 20, the condemnation Jesus had of the church was "thou sufferest" her to teach this doctrine. The word means "tolerate." They were allowing her to teach such things. There are two great dangers the church faces. One is going too far to the left (liberty) and the other is going to the right (legalism). Everything is not wrong, but we must never forget that everything is not right. The church can never allow this attitude to exist. The church must be able to be distinguished from the world.

Jesus gives a stern warning. He says He will cast her on a bed of suffering and will make those who commit adultery with her suffer intensively unless they repent. Jesus stated He would strike her children dead. In other words the children of this false prophetess, those who had been begotten by her doctrine, will be killed with death. No doubt, this means the second death, the casting of the ungodly into the lake of fire (Rev. 20:14, 21:8). With this in mind, those who have committed the immoral acts must repent. Repentance means to make a change and correct our behavior and turn from our sins.

We need to realize the qualities the church is being praised for in verse 19 are very enviable. Many Christians today lack these very qualities in their lives. Just because they have so many good things going for them does not excuse them from their faults.

It would appear that this woman Jezebel (which I am sure was not her real name) had convinced some of the believers in the church she was a prophet and taught them they could indulge in actions that were not acceptable Christian behavior and not be afraid of the ultimate consequence. It seems she had convinced these Christians to join in the trade guilds and indulge in these festive dinners. The sexual sin Jesus speaks of could be figurative, implying spiritual infidelity, a metaphor that was used throughout the Old Testament. When Christians in Thyatira partook of meat offered to idols, they figuratively, as the bride of Christ, became adulterous. However, the fact is the church had lowered its standards in spiritual areas and sooner or later was bound to lower them in the areas of morality.

ADMONITION

This letter was an eye opener to some good people who were caught up in this movement. Those who keep the teachings of God and do the will of Christ will overcome. As in each of the letters, Jesus ends this letter with a final word of exhortation. "To he that overcometh, and keepeth my works unto the end, to him will I give power over the nations..." Those who are preserved in the faith, they are now promised that Christ Himself will share with them His Messianic authority. Just as Jesus rules over the nations, so too, all those who are His will reign with Him. What words of encouragement that must have been to those who were deeply entrenched in paganism. They would be greatly encouraged with the promise they will receive one of the greatest privileges of all-ruling with Christ.

Not only will these Christians rule with Christ, He gives them something much better. "And I will give him the morning star" (v. 28). In Revelation 22:16, Jesus says, "...I am the root of David, and the bright and Morning Star." Therefore, Jesus not only promises this struggling church they will reign with Him, but they will be given the greatest treasure of all, Himself.

APPLICATION

The application for us from this letter is straightforward. Jesus warns us not to tolerate people in our midst who attempt to lead us into making unholy compromises with the world around us. As followers of Christ we can never make peace with the world, nor with the teachings of false doctrines, whether it be to secure a job or because of a desire to participate in cultural or civic activities.

While we must be willing to make sacrifices in such situations, and while we must be willing to receive the scorn of men for being followers of Christ, let us never forget what Jesus Himself promises us. Since He alone possesses all authority, not only will He crush His enemies and all them that hate Him and persecute His church, but Jesus, the Morning Star, gives us nothing less than Himself.

Therefore, "He that hath an ear, let him hear what the Spirit saith unto the churches" (v. 29).

STUDY QUESTIONS

1. Name four things the church at Thyatira was commended for:
2. What is meant by "the last to be more than the first?"
3. According to Acts 16:14-15, who was the woman from Thyatira converted by Paul?
4. Who was this woman Jezebel?
5. Why did God call her Jezebel?
6. What were her teachings leading the children of God to do?
7. What does the phrase, "and I will kill her children mean
8. What were these guilds that were causing problems to the Christians?
9. What is the application of this letter for us today?
10. Who is the Morning Star?